THE AFGHANISTAN S MAP

ZAMMIS SCHEIN

CONTRACTOR GEAR

A Collector's Guide to Weapons, Private-Purchase and Service-Issue Clothing and Equipment as Used by Civilian Contractors in Iraq and Afghanistan

Schiffer Publishing Ltd®

4880 Lower Valley Road • Atglen, PA 19310

This book is dedicated to all the brave men and women who worked as civilian contractors in conflict areas where no one in his or her right mind would have sought employment unless he or she was driven by an insatiable desire for fun and excitement and adventure … and for a fee that was proportional to the threat level in their daily work environment.

Also, this book is dedicated to my Afghan friends and colleagues as well as trainees in my courses who I had to leave behind and who I may never have a chance to meet again.

CONTENTS

Mechanix
Mechanix

BUSH ORDERS START

PREFACE

This is a comprehensive collectors' guide to OEF/OIF civilian contractors' clothing and equipment as worn in the field.

Almost all items in this book used to be my own work clothes, my equipment and my tools, or they belonged to fellow contractors who worked with me in different places at different times. Now all items comprise my private collection. *Contractor Gear* provides a comprehensive overview of what civilian contractors both in combat and in non-combat roles looked like in Afghanistan and Iraq.

For a long period of time, when I bought new "work clothes" and equipment for upcoming assignments, I did not realize that also I added new items to a constantly growing collection of contractor gear that would be presented in this book.

Since I brought virtually everything back at the end of each contract assignment and I stowed my gear for later use, it was not a big challenge to recreate scenes from the recent past and to reassemble almost all configurations of my own gear and a few colleagues' clothing and equipment. I presented them in individual chapters of *Contractor Gear*.

While Chapter 1 "The Early Days—Qubad Shah Khel, Kurram Valley, North Western Frontier, Pakistan, 2002," and Chapter 41 "PSC operator at Balad Air Force Base, Iraq, June 2014" were deliberately placed at the beginning and at the end of the book so that they mark the long period of contracting in Afghanistan and Iraq, chapters in this book are not arranged in any chronological order and individual chapters should be regarded as standalone items. Consequently, this book, as if it were a set in the mathematical sense of the word, is a collection of distinct chapters.

Since Operation Enduring Freedom (OEF) in Afghanistan was followed by Operation Iraqi Freedom (OIF) and the two Allied operations were conducted simultaneously with the involvement of a constantly changing number of civilian contractors in constantly changing roles, I did not distinguish between contractor gear worn in Iraq and in Afghanistan roughly in the same period. For example, there were two or three years when I had several consecutive assignments in both countries, where I used the same gear.

There were plenty of contract assignments when photography was my least concern. Consequently, in the overwhelming majority of cases I had to rely on my recollections about my own gear and the equipment of those who worked with me. Nevertheless, this book brings some of my own old snapshots and vidcaps from my cell phone videos back to life. These photos are presented in a film strip format.

For security and copyright reasons and for the sake of maintaining a certain level of confidentiality even after so many years, I do not use press or protocol photos of clients who I worked for, or photos of delegations that I escorted, or photos of regular military personnel who may have shown up in such pictures, since I do not intend to identify and expose them. However, I use some photos that I took myself. They are selfies in the true sense of the word, since I took them with a camcorder, or a cell phone camera held at arm's length.

Anyway, *Contractor Gear* presents private-purchase and service-issue clothing and equipment as well as weapons as used by civilian contractors in Iraq and in Afghanistan in the period between 2002 and 2014. A host of fairly detailed photographs in this book show my collection of clothing and equipment, mainly bringbacks from Iraq and Afghanistan, where I worked in different capacities as a civilian contractor.

All firearms in the collection are legally deactivated. They are collectors' items now.

My best friend, *Tovarish Makarov* no. *РГ5686*, a fine 9 mm Soviet service pistol manufactured in 1989, was stolen in Pul-e Khumri, Baghlan Province Afghanistan by those, who were supposed to guard and protect me and my gear. Such is life. Anyway, I included a few photos of the original gun in one chapter of *Contractor Gear*.

• • •

I sincerely hope that the display of my collection of contractor gear presented in realistic configurations along with my captions and brief comments and my totally subjective recollections from here and there and my fond memories of a few places and persons would convince readers that—in sharp contrast to the general portrayal of contractors in the media and in contradiction to the widely held view in the civilian society at home, which is largely attributable to the outrageous behavior of a few private security contractors in the theater of operations—the overwhelming majority of civilian contractors in Iraq and Afghanistan were not twenty-first century gunslingers.

Undoubtedly, there were some isolated cases and the indiscriminate slaughter of local civilians as well as the horrific abuse of power by a few may explain why the public perception of civilian contractors was so negative. However, it should be borne in mind that war is hell and not all regular troops, not all men and women in uniform acted like knights in shining armor in fairy tales of our childhood, either. I do not intend to clear the somewhat tarnished reputation of a few contractors in Iraq, or in Afghanistan, but we should secretly admit to ourselves, that "much worse happened at sea."

While I know that it is impossible to dispel the mercenary myth as a whole, the diversity of configurations of clothing and equipment as presented in *Contractor Gear* should prove in how many useful roles civilian contractors were employed in Iraq and Afghanistan.

I deliberately use the term "civilian contractor," since I do not wish to go into any terminological discussions about "private security contractors," "private military contractors," "DoD civilians," private security companies, risk management firms, etc. In one way or another, all of them worked "over there."

I did several tours myself. In the first few years, I was an escort interpreter and I worked with VIPs in Afghanistan and Iraq. Subsequently, I worked as an instructor and then as a teacher in Afghanistan. My self-assumed mission in Afghanistan was to "win the hearts and minds of local people" and virtually all civilian contractors I met, or I heard of, worked hard on the betterment of the lot of local people. They did not spend their days ramming innocent peoples' cars off public roads, nor did they machine gun pregnant women and young children on a daily basis for fun. If, however, any terrorist, or insurgent, or religious fanatic was asking for trouble, he or she could find it easily. I could have been particularly lucky, but the vast majority of contractors who I worked with were highly skilled, experienced and brave men and women. They were hard-working and highly dedicated people who performed their duties with distinction and honor. They worked in the theater of operations under extreme conditions for proportionally high salaries.

The clothing and equipment of brave warriors who worked on security details differed significantly from the gear of fork lift operators, who spent their time on a relatively safe military base, or a depo, or from the clothes and the equipment of truckers who ventured out far beyond the perimeter of their base and who had contact with the—frequently hostile—local population on a daily basis. Nevertheless, all civilian contractors shared virtually the same risks and challenges in a highly volatile and dangerous environment.

The quantity of contractor gear that may be required for a three-month field assignment in Afghanistan may be gauged on the basis of my photos in film strips in Chapter 42. Those pictures were taken in 2011 on the day of my redeployment from Afghanistan. The fork lift truck in one of the snapshots carries a suitcase of personal items and souvenirs as well as a host of sealed crates and cargo bags. Quite a lot of the items in them are displayed in this book. The total weight exceeded 600 lb.

ACKNOWLEDGMENTS

This book would have never been produced without the valuable help of a few great people. I salute those who helped and encouraged me.

Special thanks to my muse, namely Kati, my wife.

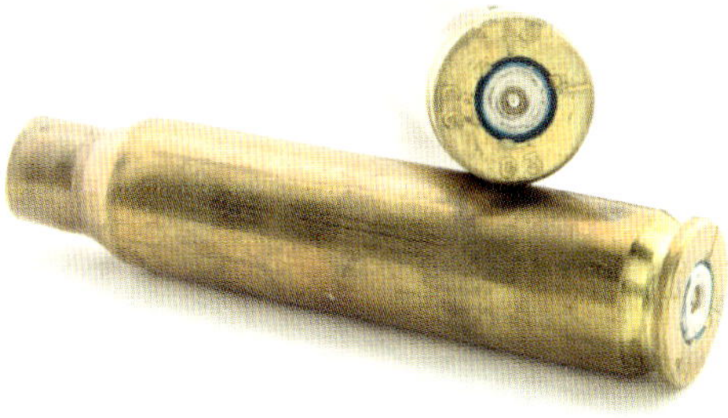

INTRODUCTION

"EOD dogs at the gate and at forward guard posts ... put their asses on the line on a daily basis ... nevertheless, they enjoyed what they were doing and they tried to 'look on the bright side of life,' exactly the same way the song in Monty Python's *Life of Brian* recommended it. So did I.

Perhaps they intuitively knew that we were kindred spirits in a roundabout way. Every time I was leaving the base ... and I walked past them at the outermost guard post, I had the impression that they were wagging their tails good-bye and I definitely knew they whispered 'see you in hell tonight' to me. We had roughly equal chances to make that rendezvous."

— Excerpts from *Zarbalistan: The Traveler's Ultimate Guide to Ariana,* by Zammis Schein.

My interest in contractor gear started with my first trips to Afghanistan and then to Iraq. Over a period of ten years and in the course of several tours in different war zones I worked as a civilian contractor either as an escort interpreter with VIPs, or as an instructor of local military and police personnel, or as a trainer of local contractors to the military, or to the government of their own nation. Undoubtedly, I reached the high watermark in my career when I received a generous grant and I taught a women's empowerment course in a girls' school that I established in scenic Pul-e Khumri, Baghlan Province, Afghanistan in 2011.

I had the privilege to work with quite a few professionals whose skills and expertise as well as bravery made all the efforts of their fellow contractors in non-combat roles possible and sustainable. I salute those heroes.

Also, in a few isolated cases I had the misfortune to work with some short-sighted, incompetent, idiotic, and ignorant people who were supposed to fund and supervise my assignments and training projects, or to guard and protect me in the theater of operations, but who turned out to be my worst enemies. I hope one day they will get what they deserve.

• • •

I hope, similarly to my previous militaria book, namely *Soviet and Mujahedeen Uniforms, Clothing and Equipment in the Soviet–Afghan War, 1979–1989*, which was published by Schiffer in 2016, all militaria buffs, collectors, reenactors, airsoft warriors, wargamers, and military historians will find *Contractor Gear* a reasonably detailed, interesting and informative illustrated guide.

I must reiterate what I have stated earlier: I am not an expert, nor is my collection complete. Anyway, I was at the right place and at the right time to build a collection of contractor gear. All I had to do to write this book was to open my "war chest," namely to pull my work clothes and equipment from storage. If I had been a civilian contractor chimney sweeper in Iraq, or Afghanistan, this book would have been written about a chimney brush and one set of pitch black tattered work clothes with a thick layer of soot on it. Luckily, this was not the case.

Most contractors I knew bought their own gear. At least, I bought mine.

There was only one case when I was ordered to wear clothing supplied by a client. Now, in hindsight, I think it was a funny story on par with a medieval farce. What happened was that in the middle of November, 2008, I arrived on a military transport aircraft from Kabul to Mazar-e Sharif. I was working on an Afghan interpreter training contract and I happened to be traveling with the new rotation of troops in the Hungarian-led PRT in Pul-e Khumri, Baghlan Province. The Chief of Staff of the PRT was on the tarmac to receive his new troops when the cargo ramp of the Lockheed C-130 was lowered. I was among the first passengers to leave the plane and all he could see in the twilight was the silhouette of my MICH helmet, which was quite different from the venerable Soviet-style steel pot helmets of his own men. For reasons still unbeknownst to me, he assumed I was some high-ranking US visitor and he snapped to attention right in front of me. In his broken English he welcomed me and he was about to lavish me with some niceties when I told him in our common native language: "You've got the wrong person, pal."

I did not mean to be impolite, let alone condescending, I did not even know who he could have been. However, all this happened in the presence of new troops who were about to serve under his command and he managed to make an ass of himself within five seconds upon their arrival. Obviously, he was gravely insulted. He did not make a scene, but next morning, when I had settled down at his base and I checked in with the commander, the chief of staff unleashed the sergeant major in the commander's office to convey his personal order: I had to wear his nation's uniform on his base. I confess, I committed high treason. I did not even bother to rip open the sealed plastic wrap of a full set of his uniform, but I returned it untouched when my contract expired. Since I was not under his command, the worst thing that he could do to me was that he did not return my greeting when I stumbled into him in the men's room.

As far as the selection of gear for an assignment is concerned, an individual contractor's choices may be determined by a multitude of different factors, including someone's dedication to, or his/her total disregard for quality, durability and prestige, or the budget that is available for the procurement of clothing and equipment. Consequently, an individual contactor's gear could comprise a mixed bag of everything at any given point in time.

However, the harsh realities of life teach everyone that no matter how dirty, torn, or damaged your clothes and your equipment may be, no matter how much surface rust, or greasy grime mixed with desert sand may have accumulated on your weapon, everything must be fully functional and readily available at all times.

Early in my career I acquired a taste for quality that only the best brands and genuine items can offer. I remember in 2011 the commander of a PRT base visited me in my newly assigned residence, namely a converted twenty-foot living container, soon after I settled down on his base. He was a bit surprised to see two different helmets on the top of my locker. He asked whether they were replicas for airsoft. My answer sobered him up: "when your ass is on the line on a daily basis and when other people's lives and the success of your mission may depend on your equipment, you do not toy around with replicas, or substandard quality items."

Actually, all items presented in *Contractor Gear* belong to the high-end category of contractor gear.

While I am not advocating any brands at all, especially not brands that obviously also target the civilian market of airsoft warriors, or reenactors with a modest budget, I found it quite interesting that seemingly perfect replicas of genuine US, German, and British service uniforms and equipment that are manufactured in oriental countries under brand names that are most frequently shunned even by serious airsoft warriors and reenactors, actually filled the aisles and shelves of PX stores on military bases in Iraq and in Afghanistan.

I would not have used a commercially available light cotton ripstop uniform instead of a service-issue flame-proof outfit myself, but I saw quite a few contractors on field duty while donning cheap stuff, e.g. bandanas, or jackets and even gloves fashioned from polyamide textiles. Nevertheless, I must admit that, statistically speaking, most of them got away with it.

If, however the proverbial shit hits the fan, even a sizzling hot, spent heavy machine gun casing may leave an ugly burn mark on these fashionable items, not to mention the devastating effects of a flash fire inside the hull of an APC.

I never used cheap stuff. Especially in the latter part of my spectacular career in Afghanistan, I preferred loose-fitting local Afghan clothes worn over a combination of service-issue US, or German military uniform items and I used high-end commercial tactical gear. My outfit helped me blend into the local environment. The combination of local civilian clothes on top of US military gear turned out to be a winning combination in more than one case.

• • •

All photographs taken for this book are of genuine service-issue, or private-purchase items in my own collection. All types of ammunition and weapons presented in this book were made inert and deactivated in accordance with the law so that they can never be made to fire again.

Zammis Schein
2016

01. The Early Days: Covert Search and Destroy Mission in Qubad Shah Khel, Kurram Valley, North Western Frontier, Pakistan, 2002

CWU-27/P Nomex flight suit, sage green, worn with service-issue brown T-shirt. M4A1 carbine with a detachable carry handle, a rail interface system (RIS), detachable handguard panels on the bottom and the right hand side, leaf sight for the M203 grenade launcher on the top rail and a flashlight with a tactical push for momentary-on/twist for constant-on tailcap switch on the left hand side (not visible in the photo). The "sling, small arms" is attached to the front sight post and the rear sling swivel on the buttstock. The *Black Banner* bears the *Shahada* in the *Nasq* calligraphic style. (For further details, see Chapter 43)

Load Bearing Vest with a steel locking carabiner, which has a threaded lock safety. M4 magazine pockets on the LBV hold two 30-round magazines each. The padded belt has hand grenade pockets, a one-quart canteen pouch, pistol mag pouches, and 40 mm grenade pouches for a M203 under-barrel grenade launcher, which is not mounted on the M4A1 in the picture.

Close-up photo of the "ball & socket" interface between the frame and rucksack belt.

MOLLE Rucksack with Frame (rear view)

Modular Lightweight Load-carrying Equipment
The Modular Load System consists of two main components: the modular pack system and the load-bearing vest, which is attached to the padded rucksack belt. The Full Rucksack Load consists of the load-bearing vest (LBV), the butt pack, the patrol pack, the rucksack with the side sustainment pockets, and the sleep system carrier mounted on the frame.

Close-up photo of the "ball & socket" interface on the rucksack frame (detail).

Pro-Tec Fullcut Helmet

The first known photographs of the Pro-Tec fullcut helmet that military censors cleared and released for publication were photos of DELTA operators participating in Operation Just Cause in Panama in 1989. Twelve years later, at the beginning of my fledgling career as a contractor to the military, I bought my Pro-Tec fullcut helmet in a sports shop.

Little did I know then that in less than a year the *Blackhawk Down* movie would make the "Protec", although a significantly different and later helmet model, world famous among movie goers and militaria fans alike. Pro-tec helmets, mainly the skateboard helmet, showed up on civilian contractors' heads in Afghanistan and in Iraq.

While the venerable M1 steel pot and the PASGT, namely the "Fritz," or the "Kevlar" helmet offered a much higher level of ballistic protection than the full-face, hockey-style Pro-tec, a plastic helmet, especially a lightweight skateboard helmet was a logical choice for anyone working on assignments where the smaller and lighter, but still bump-proof Pro-tec offered much greater mobility in close quarters and a clearer view of extremely complex and volatile situations around us.

Alas, in the line of duty my good old fullcut Pro-Tec helmet got damaged beyond repair in Al Hillah, Iraq. Subsequently, I used a sand-color Pro-Tec skateboard helmet in Afghanistan and I loved it. The vent holes on top of the newer helmet were covered with a fine mesh, which kept half of the sand and all small insects and foreign objects from entering. Nevertheless, I replaced my long-lost Pro-Tec fullcut helmet just for nostalgia's sake with a virtually identical, but recently made one, when I stumbled onto it in the new German PX store in Mazar-e Sharif in April 2011. I mounted a Picatinny tactical rail on it so that I can carry my helmet cam. It's too bad, that I've had only one opportunity to use my replacement fullcut Pro-Tec so far.

Anyway, I realized that my field modified and highly upgraded US Combat Vehicle Crewman's (CVC) helmet was best suited for my taste and to my purposes. I admit, it is a totally subjective issue … just like the selection of any other item of contractor gear.

Pro-Tec fullcut helmet with
BOLLE Tactical Safety Goggles.

BOLLE Tactical Safety Goggles.

Pro-Tec fullcut helmet
with helmet cam on
Picatinny rail (front view).

Pro-Tec fullcut helmet
with helmet cam on
Picatinny rail (rear view).

Pro-Tec fullcut helmet with
helmet cam on Picatinny rail
(inside view).

Drop Leg Holster and 9 mm Beretta M9 Pistol
The drop-leg holster has an adjustable belt hanger, two adjustable leg straps and a magazine pouch. The holster comes with an adjustable thumb break.

Empty drop leg holster, the thumb break is open, the snap fasteners are clearly visible and the Velcro safety strap is folded down.

An old mag and two brand new M9 magazines in the original wrap.

An old and used M9 mag. With the passage of time, the parkerized finish wears off.

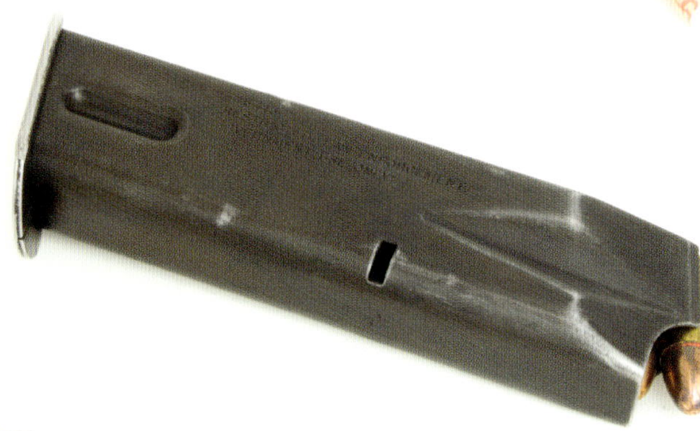

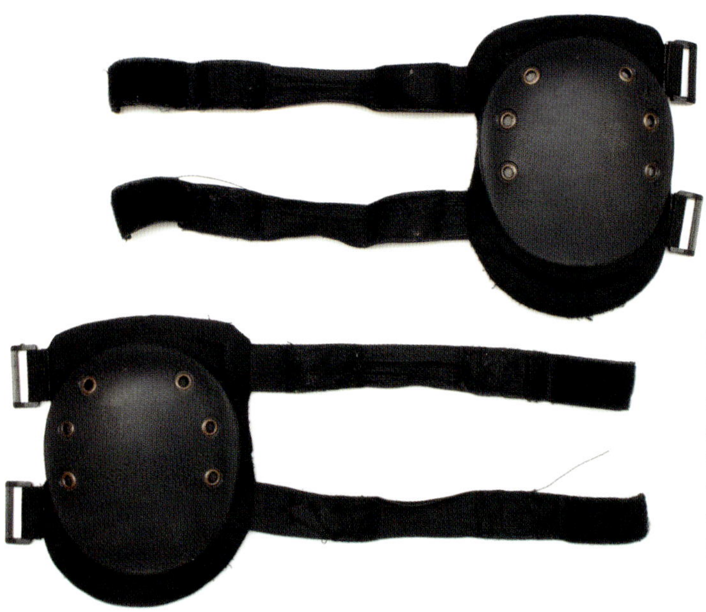

Knee Guards

The gel filled knee pads protect the knees against impact injury from falling on rough, or hard surfaces, or hitting obstacles: e.g. they protect the knee caps of a taller person who is assigned to one of the rear seats, would inevitably bump into the front seat frame in a Humvee.

Jungle Boots
The jungle boots have Panama mud-clearing outsoles, black Cordura uppers and a speedlace-and-eyelet lacing system. Screened water drain eyelets placed on the inside near the sole permit water to drain from the boots.

Some civilian contractors had a military background and also a set of USGI dog tags. Others had a set of dog tags made for themselves. And there were quite a lot who could not care less.

Close-up View of One Dog Tag on the Shoe Lace
I have always worn one tag and a small amulet taped together on a bead chain around my neck and I put the other dog tag either in a small zippered pocket inside my rigger's belt, or on the shoe lace in one of my boots. Just in case ...

02. Santa Claus Day: ISAF Base at Kabul International Airport (KAIA), 2008

Early in the morning on December 6, 2008, which was a bright sunny day, I left the ISAF base at Kabul International Airport (KAIA) for a low-profile trip to town. My mission was to meet a distinguished Afghan gentleman in his residence.

My client made the necessary arrangements and I casually walked out a side gate. I mingled in the huge crowd outside the perimeter fence virtually unnoticed and I met my trusted Afghan colleague, who was about to drive me around in a burgundy red Toyota Corolla.

I was wearing my local Afghan clothes to blend into the crowd. Under my loose-fitting *shalwar kameez* and a *patoo*, namely a thick shawl, I was wearing a pair of desert combat boots, flame resistant underpants, an *"ekwacks"* Level-2 brown-colored turtleneck top and matching drawers, a heavy duty nylon rescue rigger belt with a few absolutely essential items on it, and an ACU plate carrier harness with the heavy Kevlar inserts. An "admin" pouch was mounted on the MOLLE plate carrier. My *pakol* hat was lined with half-moon shaped aramid panels that I had removed from the shoulder protectors of a liberated German flak vest.

Everything went off without a hitch, I managed to sneak back through the same gate with the assistance of a representative of my client.

Upon my return to my living container, I took my loose-fitting Afghani clothes off when there was a knock on the door. The same representative of my client returned. With the widest grin in the whole world on his face, he summoned me to the square outside my container block. I quite forgot that I had taken my outer garments off and I went with him.

It was December 6, i.e. Santa Claus Day and two Dutch soldiers dressed up like *Sinterklaas*, i.e. Santa Claus and as *Zwarte Piet* (in English: Black Peter), who is supposed to be Santa's faithful companion in Dutch folklore. They were distributing candies to all the people who they stumbled into along their route through the base.

Under the compelling circumstances the two Dutch warriors had to settle for a substitute for the flying reindeer that pulls Santa's sleigh in all western children's fantasy world. Thus, they were accompanied by a handsome Afghan *"khar"* on that great day.

Santa Claus Encounter in Undergarments
Extended Cold Weather Clothing System (ECWCS) Level-2 "polyprop" brown-colored turtleneck top and matching drawers, Swiss Army Knife in its ACU pouch as well as a GPS navigation device carried on a heavy duty nylon rescue rigger belt, Plate Carrier Harness, ACU pattern with NKA (No Known Allergies) and blood type patches as well as an Admin Pouch.

Close-up view of the plate carrier harness, ACU pattern with NKA and *zero positive* blood type patches, INOVA red LED light on the right shoulder strap, GrimLoc spring-loaded locking D-ring on the other side, carabiner on MOLLE webbing as well as an admin pouch in matching ACU digital camouflage.

My white *shalwar kameez* is a masterpiece by the local tailor. The loose-fitting *shalwar* is placed on top of the *ek-waks* "polyprops" drawers for size comparison.

"Anti-exposure" (flame resistant) aramid fiber underpants.

Waist section of the flame resistant underpants (detail).

Plate Carrier Harness, ACU Pattern
I asked a local tailor to transfer the buckles from the back plate to the front panel to make buckling and unbuckling the plate carrier easier. It's not just a matter of taste. There may be hectic moments when doffing the plate carrier immediately may be necessary and fiddling around with a plastic buckle on the rear panel may waste valuable seconds.

Foliage green GrimLoc spring-loaded locking D-ring on the shoulder harness. The GrimLoc is a lightweight replacement for heavy-duty metal mountaineer's carabineers. The GrimLoc is perfectly suited for connecting gear that may require quick and easy one-handed access.

Full-width flaps with hook & loop fasteners on plate pockets both in the front and the back panels to hold ballistic plates.

The trauma plates are inserted into pockets in the back of the vest as well as on the front of the plate carrier harness. They absorb the kinetic energy of a bullet impact, or a high-velocity projectile, like shrapnel, and they are designed to reduce the blunt trauma transferred to the human body.

A Level 4 Trauma plate stops one hit of a 7.62 x 39 mm rifle/machine gun round and would easily stop multiple hits of lesser threats, provided that individual hits have some space between them. I wrapped the lower edge and the corners in soft padding to protect the plates and the carrier alike.

Admin Pouch. It has a Velcro panel to secure an ID patch, or other Velcro backed patches. The utility pouch will hold a mobile phone, light sticks, a flash light, a pocket knife, or a spare pistol magazine, while the two flat pockets can hold a pen and documents, or a box of small cigars.

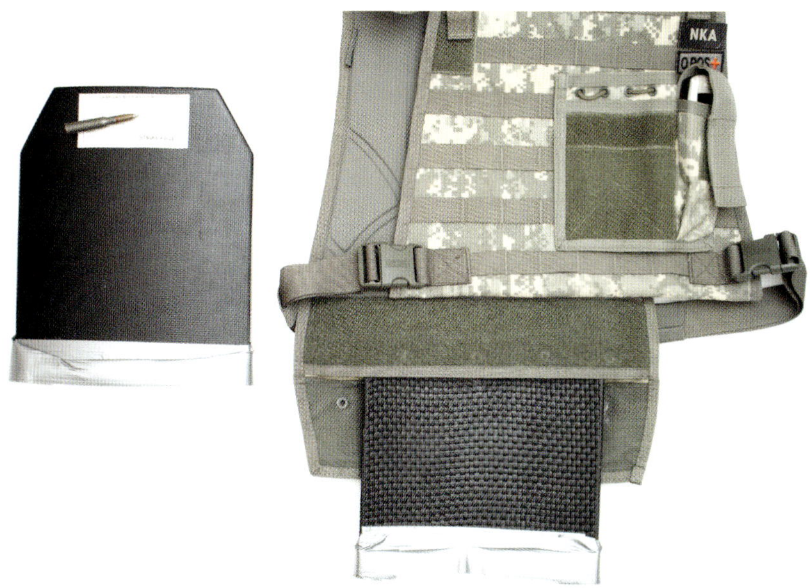

MOLLE webbing for attaching pouches, holsters or accessories.

Heavy-duty drag handle on the rear panel.

The Rescue Rigger Belt is made of 1¾" wide heavy-duty webbing and has steel hardware for complete reliability. A Velcro strip on the back of the belt is used to adjust it according to the waist size of the wearer as well as to secure the belt-end down. The "V ring" in the front, which is held by a Velcro retainer strap, accepts a carabiner for towing a wounded man out of harm's way, or making an emergency ascent or descent as the case may be. It will come as no big surprise to anyone that it fits all standard BDU belt loops on US uniforms.

Desert Combat Boots, size 12W;
the best boots I've ever had.

I always carried a boot knife, a razor sharp small knife with a flat handle in a similarly flat scabbard. I could hide it easily under my trousers on the inside of my left ankle. Since I am right handed, I could have drawn it fast. Luckily, I've never had to use it in anger.

Boot knife.

Desert Combat Boots (overhead view).

The same pair of boots were drying in my room over the electric heater after a full-day field trip in freezing mud and slush in the winter of 2008. The boots always remained water-proof and comfortable even under the most extreme conditions.

Coyote brown watch protector with Velcro closure (inside view) and hand-held GPS navigation device.

"Their captors had taken everything valuable away from them. The civilian was still unconscious, but it did not prevent the headhunters from emptying his pockets and stealing his gear. He lost everything, including his Omega Moon Watch along with the padded canvas protector around it ..."

"Where the dirt road forked, there was a Lada Niva Soviet-made 4WD lodged in between a tree and a boulder. The driver and his comrade must have been shot from behind. The hatch door was riddled by gunfire, both men's brains were strewn across the inside of the windshield, which was also penetrated by a few stray bullets. A pool of blood had gathered on the black rubber floor mats. A cloud of pesky flies congregated in the compartment. He tried not to dip his hands in blood, or brains, or whatever the slimy stuff on the steering wheel and the dashboard was and he jerked the stiff body of the driver out.

The driver landed on his side in the fine dust and gravel with a blunt noise. The sleeve of his loose shirt was shifted upwards and surprisingly an Omega Speedmaster Professional, a Moon Watch was strapped on his wrist. BINGO!"

— Excerpts from *Zarbalistan: The Traveler's Ultimate Guide to Ariana*, by Zammis Schein.

Coyote brown watch protector with an open flap.

03. Civilian Dental Surgeon on a Short-Term Contract in Afghanistan

Scrubs are the hygienic, loose-fitting shirt and trousers worn by surgeons and hospital personnel in a clean environment. Scrubs may be any color, most frequently white, or light blue, or hospital green.

Civilian doctors, consultant physicians and surgeons as well as clinical nurses worked on short-term contracts and saved lives and provided much needed front-line medical care in Afghanistan and Iraq.

T-shirt and ACU Digital Camouflage Medical Scrubs
Medium-blue disposable surgical gloves and non-woven surgical cap, the ISAF ID is on a white bead chain and is kept in the left breast pocket

The ARMY T-shirt is a part of the Improved Physical Fitness Uniform (IPFU). Also, a black dog tag ball chain is visible. A 64-inch long MOLLE Lashing Strap doubles up as a nylon webbing belt with a Fastex buckle. MOLLE Lashing Straps are originally intended for lashing additional gear to a MOLLE Rucksack, or anything with Pouch Attachment Ladder System (PALS) webbing.

Tan suede desert combat boots with Panama soles.

04. Teacher in an Afghan Girls' School, Pul-e Khumri, Baghlan Province, 2011

Oversized jean shirt, covert ballistic vest under T-shirt, *Pakol* hat with Kevlar insert, ISAF ID neck pouch, shoulder holster, riggers belt, multi-tool on lanyard, telescopic baton, IFAK pouch and trauma plate in teacher's bag, loose-fit, heavy-duty cotton duck carpenter pants.

This snapshot was taken moments before I walked out of the massive steel gate of the PRT base where I was staying during my girls' school program in Pul-e Khumri, Baghlan Province in 2011.

Every morning I took a taxi to the other side of town where my "school" was. Every day I wore either local clothes to blend into the crowd in the market and in the street, or—similarly to a host of local Afghan men—I wore a mix of western-style civilian clothes and local accessories. However, I always wore concealable body armor and flameproof undergarments. Since I did not want to expose myself too much, I kept my ISAF ID neck pouch as well as my self-defense equipment and my individual weapon under my loose-fitting outer garments. *Tovarish Makarov* in its shoulder holster makes a noticeable bulge on the left side of my shirt.

Concealable "Custom Made" Bulletproof Vest.

The XXL jean shirt fits slightly oversized, but it is intended for a slouchy fit.

A customized German Bundeswehr fragmentation vest. It is a "liberated" item, which was converted into concealable body armor by means of the removal of the neck and shoulder panels. The ballistic inserts are made of fifteen layers of aramid fabric and offer fragment and anti-stab protection. The *Bundeswehr flecktarn* camouflage pattern cover is easily removable and may be washed separately. Originally, the conversion of a readily available vest was a stop gap measure at a time when I was in a grave need of less conspicuous body armor than the PASGT frag vest. However, I came to like this vest and I used it on quite a few assignments. It was never immersed in water, nor did it get soaking wet in a storm. Consequently, it is assumed to have retained its resistance to low velocity projectiles and sharp blades throughout a long period of time. Luckily, its protective qualities have never been put to the test under fire.

Riggers Belt, foliage green, made of heavy duty 1¾" nylon webbing with a heavy duty cargo buckle. I bought it for a few Dollars in the PX at ISAF HQ, Kabul. Telescopic baton, two pistol magazine pouches in a vertical arrangement, multitool with flexible coil lanyard.

Posing with *"Tovarish Makarov"* in my customized shoulder holster. The T-shirt hides the concealable bulletproof vest.

Close-up view of my 9 mm Soviet-made Makarov pistol in a customized M12 shoulder holster.

The plate carrier under my loose fitting shirt is clearly visible in this snapshot, which was taken on the same day inside the taxicab.

Desert sand color plate carrier with trauma plates. I used the plate carrier every time I walked in the street, or I traveled in a civilian automobile, or a soft-skinned military vehicle. Just to be on the safe side, I transferred the detachable groin protector panel from a desert camo Interceptor vest to my plate carrier. Normally, I kept it tucked away under the plate carrier, but it could be folded down at a moment's notice. It was a bit cumbersome to handle it and it added some weight to my gear, but "better be safe than sorry."

My shoulder bag with a Small Arms Protective Insert (SAPI), namely one of the ceramic trauma plates removed from my Interceptor body armor, in the rear compartment. I always placed it between me and the door of the taxi cab. It could have given me some kind of protection in case of an IED explosion, or an attack. Luckily, such threat never materialized while I was traveling to or from my girls' school.

Small Arms Protective Insert (SAPI) trauma plate and a heavy duty ceramic trauma plate are placed side by side. I inserted a flexible 15-ply aramid panel, originally a shoulder protector in the German fragmentation vest, into the front side of my *Pakol* hat. It doubled up as a hat stiffener.

ISAF ID Neck Pouch
All military and civilian personnel operating in theater were issued an ISAF ID and a whole industry sprung up to manufacture ID holders that could be secured around the upper arm, or which could be worn around the neck. These pouches had zippered pockets and compartments secured with Velcro. Most important of all, the ID card had to be clearly visible at all times behind a transparent window. Most locally made sand color, or black ID pouches boasted the NATO shield, or the ISAF logo, or the US flag. Wearing one of these in the street, or in the market where I walked almost every day, while I was working deeply embedded in the local community, even if it remained concealed most of the time, would have been an open invitation for trouble. An ID pouch with the misspelled name of the country was my choice. I paid $2 for it in the local market.

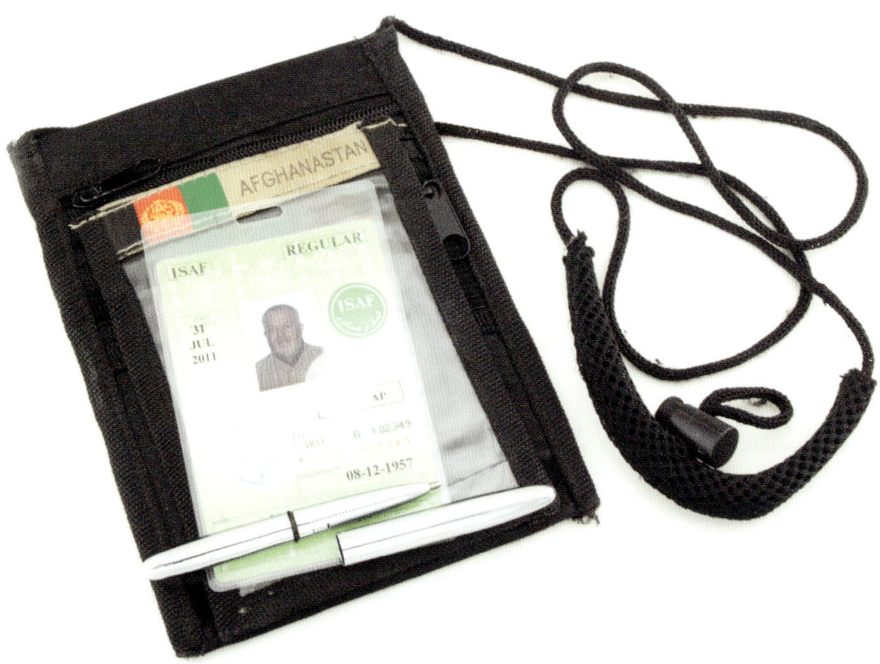

QuikClot sponge packs in sealed pouches (white, also in the carton).

Burn dressing.

Improved First Aid Kit (IFAK)
The IFAK Pouch Insert, with folding panels, is attached to the pouch with a cord. The pouch holds a tourniquet, a combat application elastic bandage kit, gauze bandage, a roll of surgical adhesive tape, a nasopharyngeal airway, i.e. a nose hose, and surgical gloves. I always carried an enhanced IFAK kit that also contained some QuikClot and burn dressing for a major emergency. QuikClot is a hemostatic product that accelerates natural clotting and stops bleeding in a very short time. Originally, it came as a powder, subsequently as a sponge pack and then as combat gauze. A used and now empty green Quikclot powder bag is also in the picture. The granules had been used as intended, and I retained the empty bag. It is a souvenir from Iraq.

Green and Blue Glow Sticks
Glow sticks give off light when two, previously isolated chemical substances in separate inner containers are mixed. When the plastic tube is flexed, the inner containers break open, their contents combine and set off a chemo-luminescent reaction and emit light as long as the chemical reaction lasts.

05. Static Perimeter Security Assignment at the Gate, Afghanistan, 2008

At the gate, wearing a PASGT helmet with a Cover, Helmet, DCU, a pair of PT-1 glasses, a PASGT vest with DCU cover, a DCU coat and trousers, an ISAF shoulder sleeve insignia, desert sand variant, a DCU visor hat in a pocket (not visible in the picture) and a pair of sage green insulated waterproof USAF flight boots.

On a bright sunny December day on a PRT base in Afghanistan, I accompanied an EOD sniffer dog handler and his K9 friend on a routine static perimeter security assignment at the gate.

Four-foot HESCO bastions were stacked two units high along the narrow path that led to the gate. Drivers were ordered to leave their vehicles and the dog inspected incoming trucks inside and out.

The dog's name was *Bende-goose*. He was a German Shepherd and we made great friends instantly. The dog handler's name was *Feh-ree*. He was Hungarian. We met for the first time on that day. He borrowed a hundred bucks instantly and he never paid it back. As the old saying goes: "With a Hungarian for a friend, who needs an enemy?" It remains an unforgettable day in my life.

A few snacks from my MRE rations sealed my friendship with *Bende-goose*.

PASGT Helmet Upgrade Kit

The Personnel Armor System for Ground Troops (PASGT) was comprised of a helmet and a ballistic vest and was used by the United States military until the introduction of the MICH helmet and the Interceptor body armor.

The PASGT helmet was most commonly known by troops as the "Kevlar," or the "K-pot," while the PASGT vest was frequently referred to as the "flak vest."

The original PASGT helmet's cradle-type suspension and headband as well as the two-point chinstrap (left) were replaced with the ballistic helmet liner and suspension system (BLSS) kit featuring a seven-pad helmet liner kit and 4-point retention system (right). The upgraded PASGT helmet is significantly more comfortable, the 4-point chin strap holds the K-pot in place and the pads provide outstanding shock-absorption.

Helmet Band with Two Light Reflective Cat Eyes Sewn on the Rear Side

Rhino NVG Helmet Mount with Head Strap to mount NVGs on the helmet. The rhino mount quickly flips the night vision goggles up and down. Square-shape IR reflective combat identification markers fit into the slits in the helmet cover. The IR markers reflect infrared light when illuminated by laser aiming devices and they reflect IR light when viewed with NVGs. In one way or another, they identify friendly personnel in the dark.

Protective Glasses

The PT-1 protective glasses have interchangeable transparent, amber and brown polycarbonate lenses. They provide ballistic-fragmentation protection and they are very comfortable. A crack started in my amber lens a few years ago and is traveling upwards at a snail's pace. These lenses virtually never fog up, which is a big advantage within a confined space, like inside an up-armored civilian 4WD, or even in a Humvee.

The Rx Prescription Insert for the PT-1 makes the lives of soldiers who need prescription lenses much easier. The Rx has to be snapped onto the nose piece of the PT-1 Sunglasses.

HL1-A-TN Tactical Helmet Light with Helmet Mount

It has three white and two blue forward-looking LEDs and a blinking infrared IFF beacon on the side. The light source may be selected with two toggle switches. A pressure switch controls the intensity of the LED light

Tactical Helmet Light with three white forward-looking LEDs.

Tactical Helmet Light with two blue forward-looking LEDs.

3V Batteries for the tactical helmet light. The light operates on one battery only.

Cover, PASGT Vest, Camouflage Patter, DCU
The formal name of the vest was "Body Armor, Fragmentation Protection Vest, Ground Troops" but it was usually called the "PASGT Vest," or the "flak vest." Originally, the "flak jacket" has a woodland camouflage outer cover. However, both six-color and three-color desert camo covers were issued for the PASGT vest.

The ECWCS Level-2 brown turtleneck top worn under the "Coat, Desert camouflage pattern, combat" is clearly visible behind the collar of the flak jacket. The flak vest has two front pockets with Velcro closure (which may be reached through slits in the cover) as well as two grenade hangers. The shoulder pads are held in place with elastic webbing and snaps.

Choosing a holster is a totally subjective issue for any contractor. In an ideal situation I would prefer a concealed shoulder holster, or an open-carry chest rig cross-draw holster configuration. However, bulky body armor, especially in combination with an ammo vest, would make it virtually impossible to mount and then to reach a shoulder holster. Body armor without PALS webbing, like the PASGT flak vest, would not support a chest rig, anyway. Simply there is no room for a traditional hip holster under the flak jacket. Consequently, a drop-leg holster is the only available option. It can be reached easily and the shooter can draw his gun even in the sitting position without any difficulty. However, I admit it is not suitable for "kinetic operations" when a shooter may have to run around a lot with a heavy pistol in his thigh holster, which is wobbling and wiggling in every conceivable direction all over his thigh.

Pistol, Caliber .45, Automatic, M1911A1 in the Drop-leg Holster
This tactical thigh rig can mount holsters for different types of guns. This type of holster has an auto locking gun retention and push-button gun release mechanism.

Sage green insulated waterproof USAF flight boots.

06. VIP Escort Assignment, Al-Hillah, Iraq, 2004

PASGT helmet, black body armor with trauma pads and groin protector flap, green T-shirt, angler's vest, khaki chinos, USMC-issue hot weather combat boots

My classic–fit khaki chino pants were pretty roomy through the seat and thigh, which made this short escort assignment in Al-Hillah, Iraq quite tolerable in the scorching summer heat.

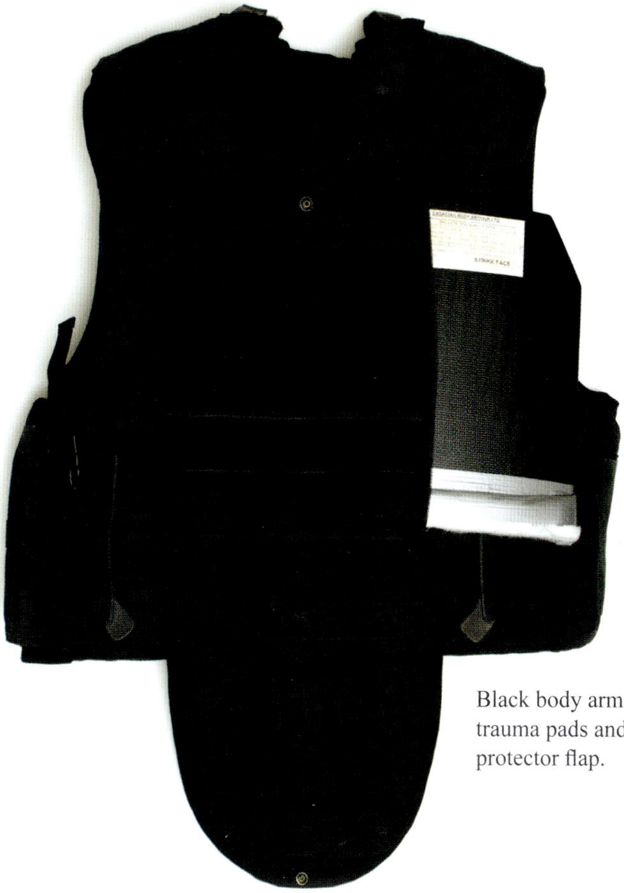

Black body armor with trauma pads and groin protector flap.

Black body armor (front view).

Black body armor (rear view).

Angler's vest.

Two-way radio acoustic coil tube headset with a push-to talk (PTT) mike and a translucent earbud. In this case the PTT switch was mounted on the Velcro-backed shoulder adjusting panel of my body armor. The radio pouch on the left hand side of the vest holds my two-way radio.

USMC hot weather combat boots proudly display the eagle, globe, and anchor emblem.

A pair of hot weather combat boots.

PASGT helmet with desert tan chin strap, light adjusting "aviator" style sunglasses.

The big advantage of my vintage light adjusting sunglasses was that I did not have to carry around more than one pair of glasses, since they darken as the brightness of the sun dictates it. When more light is encountered outdoors in the sun, they get darker. Indoors, or late in the afternoon, the sunglass lens tint gradually becomes lighter in color. Although I wore them on several field assignments and I loved them, my biggest concern was that they were not shatterproof.

07. VIP Escort Assignment in Baghdad, Iraq, 2007

A few frames captured from a video that I took from the helicopter.

In the second frame the reflection of the door gunner is clearly visible in my mirror-coated sunglasses.

In early 2007, my client visited NATO Training Mission—Iraq (NTM-I) Headquarters within the International Zone, a.k.a. the Green Zone in Baghdad. He was hosted by the deputy commander on that day. He also visited the Iraqi Military Academy in the NTM-I Forward base at Ar Rustamiyah, approximately ten miles south east of Baghdad.

Myself and two US troopers plus the helicopter crew flew alongside the VIP guest in a separate helicopter.

I wore a pair of mirrored sunglasses, my PASGT helmet without a cover, my pitch-black, heavy-duty bullet-proof vest with trauma plates in the rear and the front pockets as well as a multi-pocket angler's vest with all sorts of goodies including an enhanced first aid kit, in the pockets. Two and a half years earlier I happened to do another VIP escort job in Iraq for a different client in exactly the same outfit, except for the sunglasses.

These are vid caps captured from a short movie that I took during a trip in an up-armored GMC truck across the Green Zone. A two-inch thick bullet-proof windscreen and similarly massive side windows as well as heavy Kevlar panels mounted on the chassis comprise an inner shell that would stop small arms ammo and rocket propelled grenades. Lots of soft-skinned vehicles were up-armored in this way.

These vid caps show Saddam Hussein's "Hands of Victory" (a.k.a. the "Swords of Qadisiyah'), monument on both sides of the dictator's parade ground. Our vehicle passed under the Victory Arch, which was originally intended to serve as a monument to the war against Iran. The enormous bronze hands are said to have been shaped after Saddam Hussein's precious hands. Rumor has it that—for authenticity's sake—the sculptor took Saddam's fingerprints so that the dictator's fingerprints can be transferred to the bronze statue.

Top Jimmie Climate Control Sunglasses
The "facial cavity seal" literally seals off the wearer's eyes from airborne debris, desert sand and dust. These glasses were the perfect choice for a place like Iraq where I needed a clear and unobstructed view of our constantly unfriendly environment. While there was a strong need for the impact protection and UV filtration features of USGI dust goggles, as an escort interpreter, I was not supposed to wear anything, but "conventional-looking" sunglasses.

Mirrored sunglasses

Iraqi M80 helmet shell, a memento of the Iraq-Iran war, purchased at the Green Zone Shopping Bazaar. Actually, it is a South Korean-produced M-76 helmet, which was based on the US M1 pattern and which was made of a ballistic nylon fibre. The helmet was sold to a lot of nations, including Iraq, where it had the M80 designation.

Thousands of captured Iranian helmets are held in a bronze net next to the wrist of each giant hand. They are said to have been collected in battlefields that were strewn thick with fallen Iranians. They create the impression that a never-ending stream of a vast variety of Iranian Army steel pots, also including World War II, and post-war British helmets and more recent Soviet-style helmets, keeps rolling out of the bronze net. In a similar fashion, thousands of war booty Iranian helmets were laid direct into the concrete road under the Crossed Swords. The row of buried helmets acts like a sleeping policeman and the sheer fact that Iraqi vehicles roll over the captured Iranian steel pots is supposed to add to the utter humiliation of Saddam's former arch enemy.

Helmets supposedly salvaged from the two "Hands of Victory" monuments were sought-after souvenirs among the liberators. In actual fact, only a small number of helmets could have been removed from the monument by allied personnel who could afford to stop by and collect a war trophy like this in the heart of Baghdad. Iranian helmets from the Victory Arch were sold by a host of dealers in the Green Zone shopping bazaar, in street markets and through even less official channels for approximately $30. Needless to say, most of them were fake. Even in the best case, they had been picked up in former battlegrounds in the desert.

I myself brought home a battered Iraqi M80 helmet. I bought it "under the counter" in the Green Zone shopping bazaar from a local trader for $10 plus a candy bar for his little son.

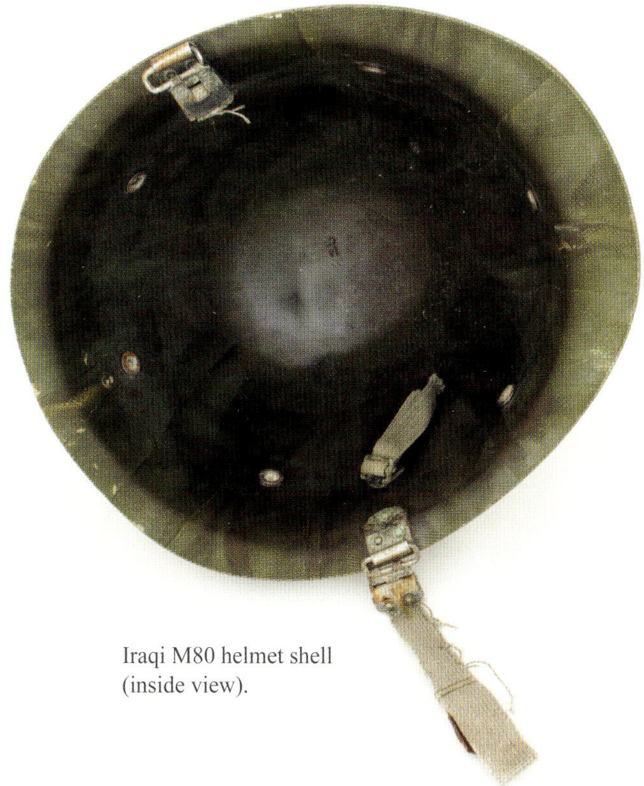

Iraqi M80 helmet shell (inside view).

Iraqi M80 helmet shell (side view).

Safe conduct pass, obverse.

Gulf War vintage Iraqi 25 Dinar Surrender Note with charging horsemen at center and Saddam Hussein at right. A Safe Conduct Pass is printed on one side and the exact replica of the Iraqi currency is printed on the other side.
Now I know that I was ripped off when I bought it from a vendor in the Green Zone bazaar. Little did I know at that time that it had nothing to do with the 2003 Allied invasion and the liberation of Iraq, since it was printed in 1991, as one of the numerous types of psychological warfare leaflets that the Allies disseminated during their Desert Storm campaign.

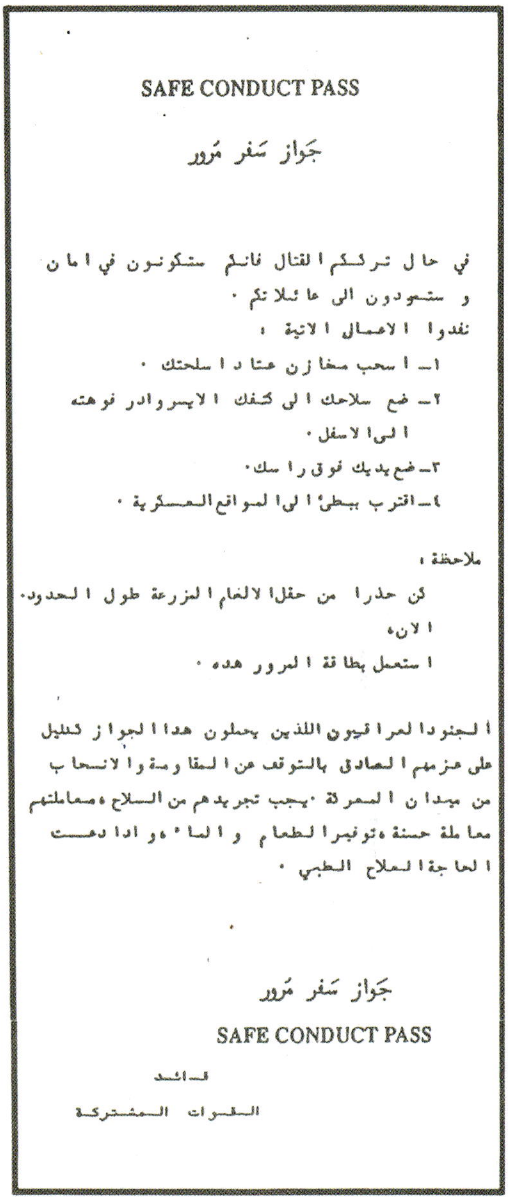

SAFE CONDUCT PASS

جَواز سَفر مُرور

في حال ترككم القتال فانكم ستكونون في امان
و ستعودون الى عائلاتكم .
نفذوا الاعمال الاتية :
١ـ اسحب مخازن عتاد اسلحتك .
٢ـ ضع سلاحك الى كتفك الايسر وادر فوهته
الى الاسفل .
٣ـ ضع يديك فوق راسك.
٤ـ اقترب ببطئ الى المواقع العسكرية .

ملاحظة :
كن حذرا من حقل الالغام المزرعة طول الحدود.
الان.
استعمل بطاقة المرور هده .

الجنود العراقيون اللذين يحملون هدا الجواز كدليل
على عزمهم الصادق بالتوقف عن المقاومة والانسحاب
من ميدان المعركة .يجب تجريدهم من السلاح ،معاملتهم
معاملة حسنة ،توفيرالطعام والماء ،و اذا دعت
الحاجة العلاج الطبي .

جَواز سَفر مُرور

SAFE CONDUCT PASS

قائد
القوات المشتركة

Safe conduct pass, reverse.

Translation from Arabic into English:

SAFE CONDUCT PASS

You do not have to die. You can be safe and return to your family and loved ones, if you cease resistance. You must follow these steps strictly.

1. Remove the magazine from your weapon.
2. Sling your weapon over your left shoulder with the muzzle down.
3. Raise your arms above your head.
4. Approach our positions slowly. Hold this pass in your hand above your head.

If you do this, you will not die. You will be treated well and you will return to your family. *Note*: Beware of mine fields along the border. Iraqi soldiers who carry this Safe Conduct Pass use it as a token of their sincere desire to cease resistance and to be removed from the battlefield. They will be disarmed, they will be treated well and they will receive food, water, and medical assistance, if they need treatment.

The Commander of the Allied Forces

A 250 Dinar note issued in 2002, the last full year of Saddam's rule, with Saddam Hussein's image on the obverse and the Dome of the Rock on the reverse. The security features of this banknote comprise a watermark with a floral pattern as well as a security strip woven into the paper, both on the left-hand field of the obverse face.

Originally, I intended to use it as a "short snorter" and I thought it would be a great idea to retain an obsolete Iraqi banknote immediately after the deposition of Saddam, inscribed by colleagues who worked together on the same contract. In the last hectic moments of our assignment I never got around to asking anyone to sign it. So I kept it exactly in the same condition as I obtained it. N.B.: The handwriting says "Khalid," which is a man's name.

A new 50 Iraqi dinar note issued by the Coalition Provisional Authority in 2003. There is a grain silo and ships in Port of Basra on the obverse and date palms on the reverse. Old banknotes were exchanged for these new ones at a one-to-one rate. I simply forgot about it and I left it in one of the many pockets of my angler's vest.

Chrome–plated AMD-65 assault rifle, the Hungarian variant of the AKM, with a hinged side-folding stock, the unique AMD muzzle brake, a perforated sheet metal handguard and a vertical foregrip, which happens to be identical to the rear grip, but mounted in a forward-looking position.

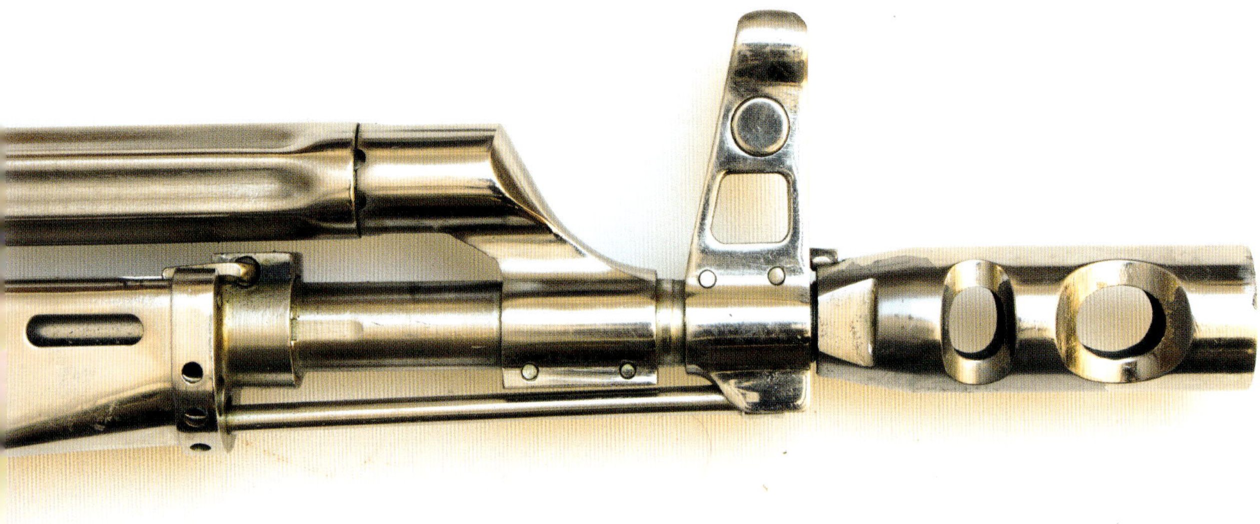

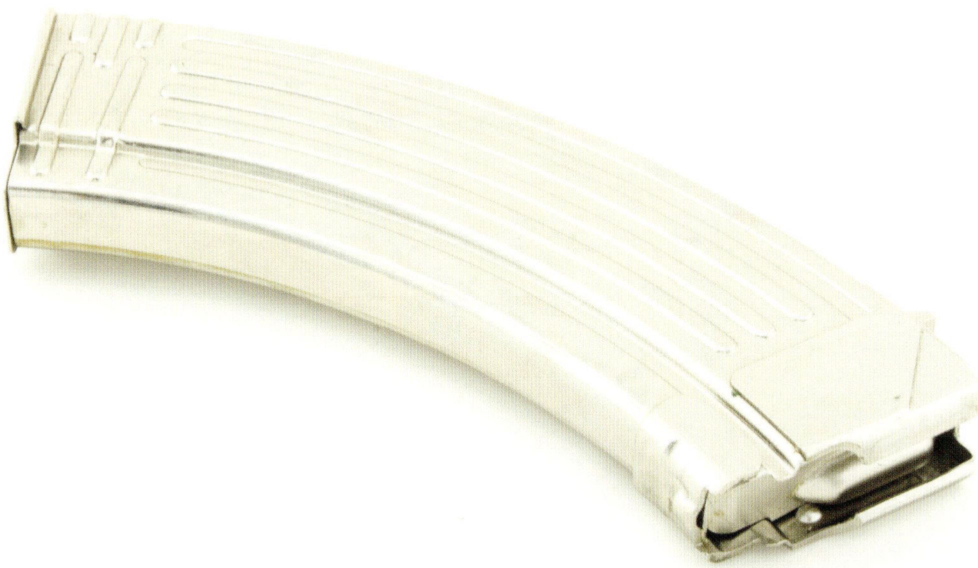

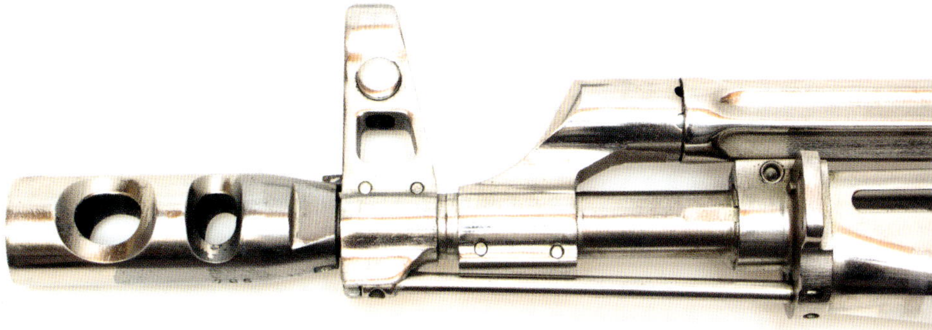

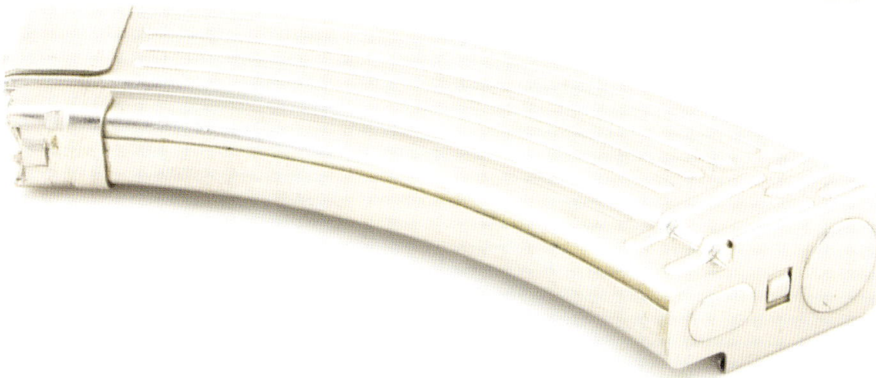

The gun was deactivated by a licensed armourer and a proper deactivation certificate was issued. The barrel was drilled in several places, the chamber entrance was pinned and welded. Also, the firing pin was destroyed.

The wooden case is painted "gunship grey" on the outside and has a high gloss black interior. The cutout in the bottom panel follows the contours of the gun. The bottom is covered with green felt. The gun is held in place by black felt pads on the inside wall of the cutout.

Chrome-plated AMD-65 folding stock assault rifle in its presentation case. No information about the former owner, or the history of the gun was available. No trace of a dedication plaque was found in the presentation box when I acquired it.

The presentation box has a small metal tag. *AMD65* is written on it in Arabic with green oil paint. There is a stamped number on the reverse side. It is not visible now, but I discovered it when I cleaned up and oiled the metal hardware on the wooden box. The hinges, the locks, and the folding handles on this wooden case are similar to those installed on Soviet army optical instrument boxes.

08. Trucking Contractor in Camp Anaconda, 2005

"IED on the left side! … two IEDs … gunfire, truck-bound … Jesus Christ, help us, oh, Lord … I am truck 5 and cannot move … please help me … I'm taking fire … 10–4? … Come back … I'm fixing to get killed, GODdam it … I cannot move … how 'bout getting your ass back here, please!"

Excerpts from a radio exchange between a wounded trucking contractor in Iraq, who was trapped in his wrecked truck … alone … with no gun and with two AK-47 bullets in his arm. He and his colleagues were abandoned by their military escort, which "pulled up out of the kill zone and established a security defensive line further down the road," while three other truck drivers in the same doomed convoy were executed in cold blood by insurgents who had staged the ambush. (2005, Iraq)

PASGT helmet, main contractor's logo neck ID holder, polo shirt, jeans, sneakers, weathered work gloves.

PASGT helmet
Truck driver's PAGT helmet with standard olive green chin strap, sunglasses.

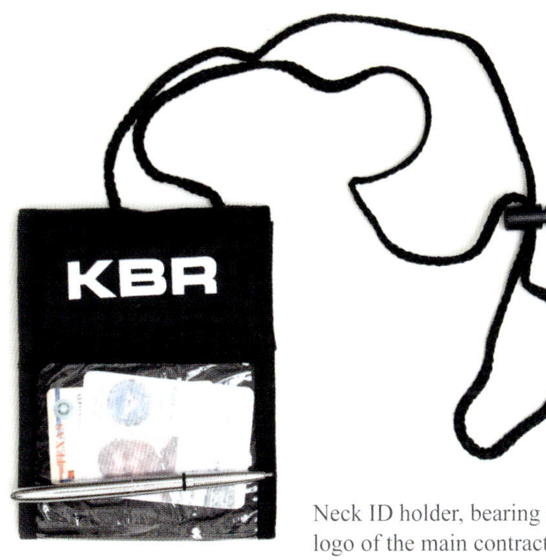

Neck ID holder, bearing the logo of the main contractor to the DoD.

Weathered work gloves.

09. Indian Sikh Truck Driver Contractor in LSA Anaconda, Iraq, 2005

A *Dastaar* is the Sikh turban and is an integral part of the Sikh culture, a sacred symbol of the Sikh faith. Wearing a Sikh turban is mandatory for Sikh men.

In both World Wars I and II, Sikh servicemen fought valiantly in the British Army and were not required to wear metal helmets over their turbans. Even now, Sikh motorcyclists in several countries are exempted from wearing a helmet over their turban, when riding a bike.

In Iraq, however, the security situation on public roads where supply convoys traveled was so bad, that occasionally common sense dictated that even Sikh trucking contractors should put their K-pot on.

Surplus CWU- 27/P desert tan fire resistant Nomex flight suit, as worn by contractors, mainly by TCNs in Iraq, checkered shirt, neon green high visibility belt worn around the waist, PASGT helmet with black helmet cover, sleeve-mounted ID holder with Camp Anaconda-DoD contractor ID card, desert boots—Wibram sole.

Orange visibility belt slung across the chest, closeup
Neck lanyard bearing the logo of the main contractor to the DoD with the contractor's ID card in a transparent plastic ID holder.

PASGT helmet with black helmet cover, worn on top of a Sikh turban made of cream color "F74" fabric.

PASGT helmet with black helmet cover.

Safety rules that made reflective "PT" (physical training) belts mandatory in the Army in a wide variety of situations and under all sorts of conditions were set forth in Army Regulations *AR 670-1: Wear and Appearance of Army Uniforms and Insignia,* and *AR 385-10: The Army Safety Program.* The same rules were rigorously enforced in case of civilian contractors as well. Neon green, optic yellow as well as orange safety vests over the clothing of civilian contractors as well as reflective belts, a.k.a. "PT" belts, around the waist, or slung across the chest of contract personnel were a common sight on army bases and military installations in Iraq and in Afghanistan alike.

By and large, reflective belts were just as popular with contractors as with regular military personnel. In other words, virtually everyone hated them from the bottom of their hearts.

Orange high visibility (PT) belt
The reflective stripe in the middle glows brightly when there is a small angle between our eyes and the light source directed toward the PT belt.

The reflective stripe in the middle appears nonreflective when we look at it from any other direction.

Neon green high visibility (PT) belt.

Side release buckle on neon green visibility (PT) belt, rear side view, closeup.

Another neon green high visibility (PT) belt with a different buckle.

10. Fork Lift Operator: Forward Operating Base Delta, Al Kut, Iraq, 2009

Short visor hard hat with safety campaign sticker, neck lanyard with plastic ID holder, high visibility vest, US Army issue, denim work wear: chambray shirt, carpenter jeans, black cowhide leather and nylon fabric waterproof duty boots, high performance work gloves.

Short visor hard hat with safety campaign sticker (side view).

Short visor hard hat with V-shaped hardening ribs (front overhead view).

High visibility vest, US Army issue, front and rear panel, flaps with hook and loop fasteners, (stenciled number on rear), inside view with label.

High visibility vest, inside view with label (detail).

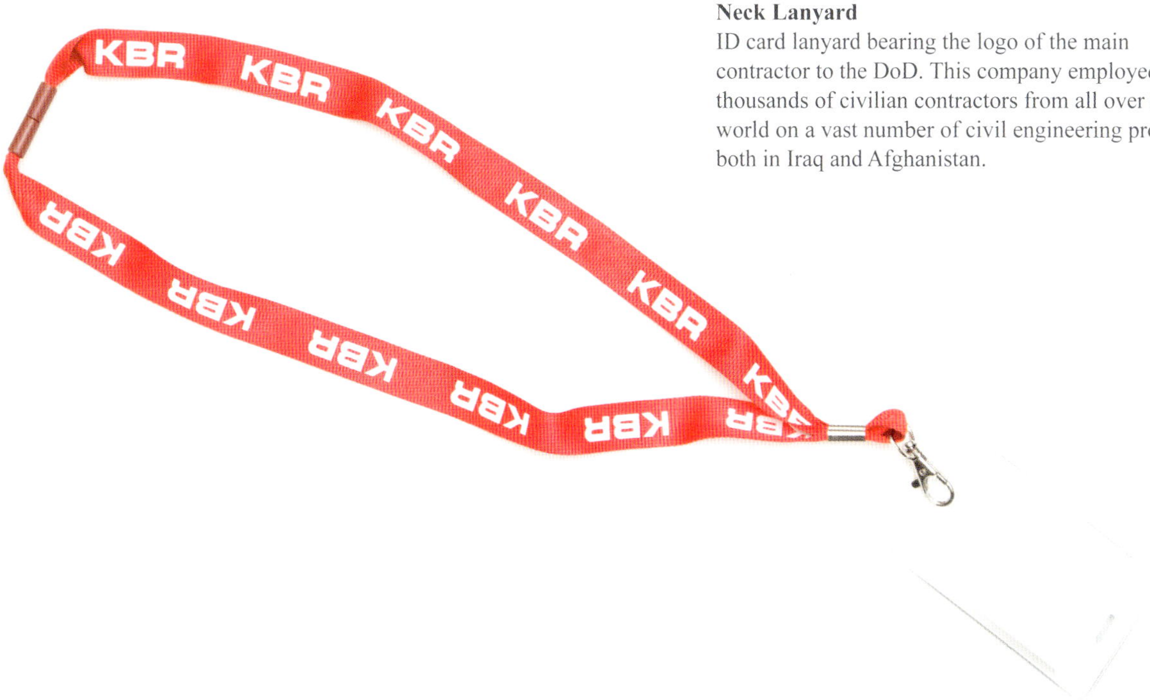

Neck Lanyard
ID card lanyard bearing the logo of the main contractor to the DoD. This company employed tens of thousands of civilian contractors from all over the world on a vast number of civil engineering projects both in Iraq and Afghanistan.

Black cowhide leather and nylon fabric waterproof duty boots, (detail).

11. Foreman at Al Asad, Iraq, 2006

Wide brim hard hat with the main contractor's safety campaign sticker, red string neck lanyard with the DoD main contractor's logo, plastic ID holder, optic yellow high visibility vest, desert boots, Panama soles, red high performance work gloves.

Wide brim hard hat with the main contractor's safety campaign sticker.

Wide brim hard hat with V-shaped hardening ribs (front overhead view).

12. Civil Engineering Contractor in Iraq Wears Theater–Made Civilian/Non-Combatant Insignia

CWU-27/P desert tan fire resistant Nomex flight suit, Interceptor body armor (IBA) with side plates in the Universal Camouflage Pattern, Improved First Aid Kit (IFAK) mounted on the vest, non-combatant insignia on the DCU cover of the Modular Integrated Communications Helmet (MICH), desert sand color Nomex flight gloves, tan suede desert combat boots with Panama soles.

This civil engineering contractor in Iraq wears a theater–made version of the civilian/non-combatant desert subdued insignia, namely the tan letters "U.S." on an equilateral triangle, printed on a matching desert sand color background and sewn onto his MICH helmet cover.

Such non-combatant insignia may, but does not necessarily denote the actual duty assignment of a civilian contractor.

The non-combatant patch may be worn centered directly above the left pocket, or on the left sleeve of the field uniform, or centered on the front of the patrol cap. Civilian contractors may wear their nametape on the right and an affiliation tape, such as "CONTRACTOR" on the left side.

Minor deviations from these regulations in terms of the placement, or the design, or even in the color of non-combatant patches occurred frequently.

The wear of uniforms by US civilians in the theater of operations is regulated by Army Regulation *AR 670-1, section 30–10 (Wear of Uniforms by US civilians).*

A theater-made version of the civilian/non-combatant desert subdued insignia.

Non-combatant insignia sewn onto the DCU cover on the Modular Integrated Communications Helmet (MICH).

Modular Integrated Communications Helmet (MICH) with DCU pattern helmet cover (side view).

Modular Integrated Communications Helmet (MICH) with DCU pattern helmet cover, the manufacturer's label and the liner pads are clearly visible (inside view).

Modular Integrated Communications Helmet (MICH) with DCU pattern helmet cover, the helmet cover Velcro mounting straps are under the liner pads (inside view).

DCU pattern MICH Reversible Woodland (DCU) helmet cover, rear side, communications flap and Velcro mounting straps (detail).

Close-up view of the DCU pattern MICH Reversible Woodland (DCU) helmet cover, rear side, communications flap and Velcro mounting straps.

Desert Sand Color Nomex Flight Gloves
The snug fitting, gauntlet style sheepskin and stretchable Aramid/Nomex flight gloves provide outstanding forearm and hand protection not only for flight crews in a cockpit, but also for ground troops in the field. The flight gloves are fire resistant, the Aramid/Nomex fabric in the glove does not melt, nor would it burn.

Theater–made civilian/non-combatant desert subdued insignia. The tan letters US on an equilateral triangle, are embroidered on a matching desert sand color background with Velcro backing. The patch is mounted on a coat, desert camouflage pattern: combat, and is worn on the left elbow.

Private-purchase civilian/non-combatant insignia worn on the rank insignia holder of the Army Combat Uniform coat. The foliage green letters US are embroidered on a black equilateral triangle and placed on an ACU camouflage background. The patch may be attached with a hook and loop fastener.

13. TCNs, or Third Country Nationals: A Mess Hall Cook

Basketball logo pom-pom hat, main contractor's ID holder, white long sleeve T-shirt, "Bear Suit" (Shirt, Cold Weather, Synthetic Fiber Pile), white carpenter's trousers, white sneakers.

TCNs, or Third Country Nationals, were contract workers recruited mainly from the Philippines, India, Pakistan, and Thailand.

Sadly enough, in the majority of cases they received lower wages and less favorable contract terms both in Iraq and Afghanistan. Also, they suffered a certain measure of discrimination at the hands of their employers and their fellow contractors alike. Nevertheless, these civilian contractors in the blue-collar workforce often found themselves in harm's way just like their colleagues from English-speaking countries.

This chapter is dedicated to a mess hall cook at the PRT base in Pul-e Khumri, Baghlan Province, Afghanistan. He worked there on successive contracts for several years.

A red pom-pom hat with a black fold up brim, which he seemed to have been wearing day and night, became his hallmark.

All I know about him is that his hard-earned salary supported more than a dozen members of his extended family in a small village in India. He was a very nice person.

***Spey* (dog in Pashto) in the School Yard Eats Pizza and Calamari Rings**

Leftover food from the mess that my friend in his hallmark pom-pom hat passed on to me in large garbage bags after dinner time gave a few stray dogs in the neighborhood around my girls' school at the other end of town a taste of western food and kept them well fed throughout my contract period.

Shirt, Cold Weather, Synthetic Fiber Pile
This first generation ECWCS (Extreme Cold Weather Clothing System) fleece jacket was nicknamed the "Bear Suit" and was intended to be worn under the Goretex Parka.

Maintenance technicians, civilian contractors from the Philippines, are cleaning my air conditioner in front of the living quarters, namely rows of modified shipping containers on the PRT base where I stayed.

A local contractor is riding a motor tricycle on the PRT base.

14. VIP Escort Interpreter in Flame-Resistant ACU Uniform in Afghanistan, 2007

Flame-Resistant Army Combat Uniform (FRACU), foliage-green t-shirt, Interceptor body armor (IBA) with Upper Arm Protectors and Side Plates, Disposable double cuff plastic restraint, Aircrew Survival/Egress Knife (ASEK), Modular Integrated Communications Helmet (MICH), Nape Protector, Streamlight Sidewinder tactical flashlight with articulating head.

Flame-Resistant Army Combat Uniform (FRACU) worn with foliage-green T-shirt. The Mandarin collar is worn up with the body armor. Otherwise, it is worn folded down.

I worked as an escort interpreter for a government minister and a US ambassador on their joint visit to Afghanistan in 2007.

I worked in full uniform. I decided to wear my flame-resistant ACU outfit to blend in with the military on the bases and on other locations that my clients visited. Needless to say, I had no military rank insignia, or any unit, or combat patches. I had my Velcro-backed name tape on the right and a "CONTRACTOR" affiliation tape on the left side.

I did not wear the civilian/non-combatant insignia, namely the black equilateral triangle with the letters "US" in it, printed on a matching digital ACU camo background, since I was not working on a US contract on that particular assignment.

The wear of uniforms by US civilians in the theater of operations is regulated by Army Regulation, *AR 670-1—section 30–10 (Wear of Uniforms by US Civilians)* in general and by the *Memorandum of HQ ISAF*, dated July 18, 2012 in Afghanistan.

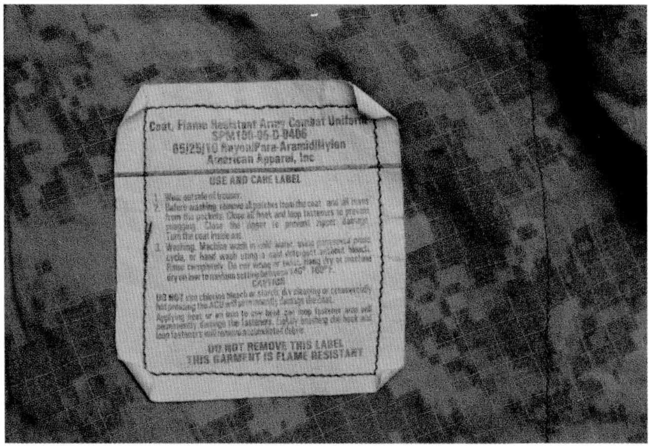

Flame-Resistant Army Combat Uniform (FRACU), a flame-retardant variant of the Army Combat Uniform.

Army Combat Uniform sleeve pocket with infrared tab, opened (right).

When I wore my ACUs, I tucked the pants into the boots and I kept my boot knife in the right hand-side calf pocket. It is clearly visible that the tip of the scabbard rubbed threadbare spots in the material.

There are calf storage pockets on both pant legs.

1 x 1 inch tabs sewn onto the left sleeve cuff of the coat and the left cargo pocket flap of the trousers are unique to FR uniforms that offer their wearers a few extra seconds of protection before the FRACU fabric combusts in case of exposure to extreme heat, like in case of an IED attack.

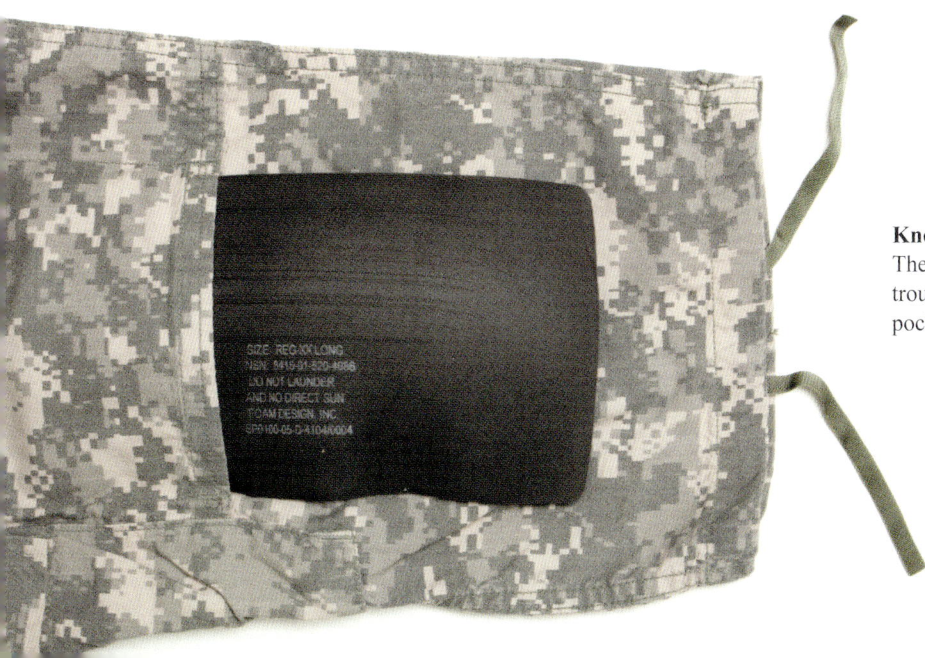

Knee Protectors
The kneepad inserts in the ACU trousers are held in a patch pocket with Velcro closure.

The Interceptor body armor (IBA) is a bullet-resistant vest comprising the Outer Tactical Vest (OTV) and two Small Arms Protective Insert (SAPI) ballistic plates. I wear size XXL. The insulated tube with the bite valve of the hydration system is attached with a GrimLock D-ring on the left-hand side. There is a disposable double cuff plastic restraint on the right.

An Aircrew Survival/Egress Knife (ASEK) in its snap closing sheath within a pocket is also mounted on the right-hand side.

Just to be on the safe side, I threaded one plastic restraint in the MOLLE webbing on my vest. I myself would prefer the employment of non-lethal methods, while everyone in the formal security detail would have used more straightforward methods to restrain an assailant. None of them carried handcuffs.

The Small Arms Protective Insert (SAPI) is a ceramic trauma plate.

Interceptor body armor (IBA) with Upper Arm Protectors and Side Plates, the hydration system with an insulated feed tube is in a matching ACU carrier. An external hydration system carrier is needed, if there is a trauma plate in the back pocket (rear view).

Interceptor body armor (IBA) with a SAPI plate in the rear compartment (rear view).

I carried an additional groin protector ballistic panel in the front SAPI compartment. Just in case …

Interceptor body armor (IBA) with an open front (outside view).

Interceptor body armor (IBA) with an open front (inside view). The groin protector in its ACU cover, which originally belonged to the vest, is folded up.

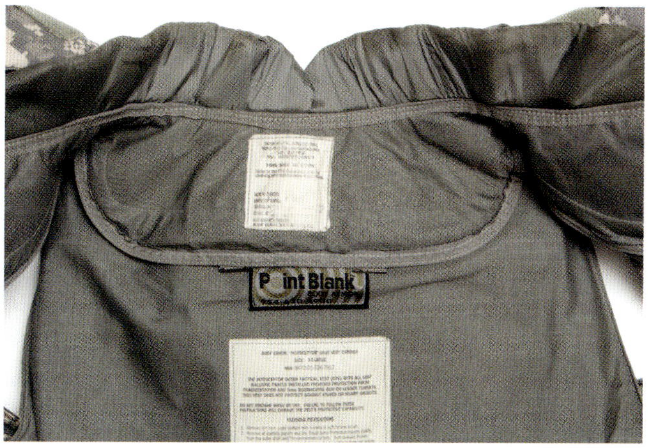

Close-up photo of the neck protector and the rear panel with the manufacturer's labels (inside view).

Aircrew Survival/Egress Knife (ASEK) has a 5" black phosphate-coated blade with a saw tooth back. The knife has a leather handle and a hexagonal pommel, which doubles up as an emergency hammer. This knife is securely retained in its snap closing sheath within a pocket of the AIRSAVE CMU-33 Survival Vest, mounted in the upside down position.

Foliage green flame resistant goatskin leather tactical gloves with knuckle protectors.

The high cut and brimless Modular Integrated Communications Helmet (MICH).

The seven-pad helmet liner kit and the four-point retention system are similar, but not identical to the upgraded PASGT helmet.

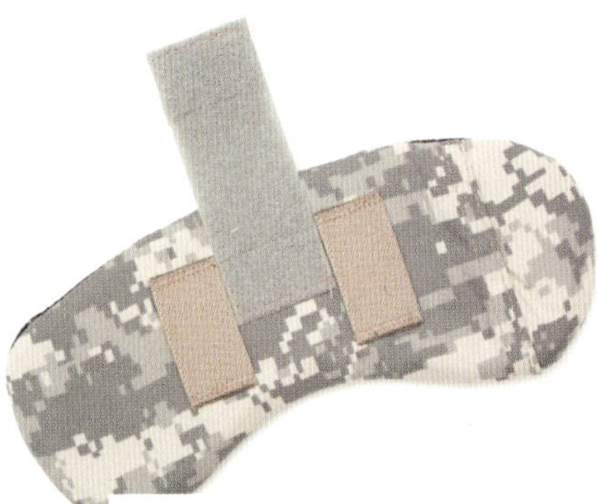

Nape Protector
The Nape Protector is a ballistic armored panel that is attached to the rear retention straps on the MICH. The Nape Protector offers additional ballistic coverage to the lower skull and the upper neck.

Nape Pad, back side, the soft fabric is in contact with the neck and the lower skull, the label is clearly visible.

A 9 mm M9 pistol in a tactical paddle holster, a coiled pistol lanyard and a spare pistol mag in an ACU pouch are carried on a heavy duty nylon rescue rigger belt.

9 mm M9 pistol in a tactical paddle holster with a coiled pistol lanyard attached to the lanyard loop, spare pistol magazines in ACU pouches.

SG-1 tactical goggles in their padded case with a zipper closure.

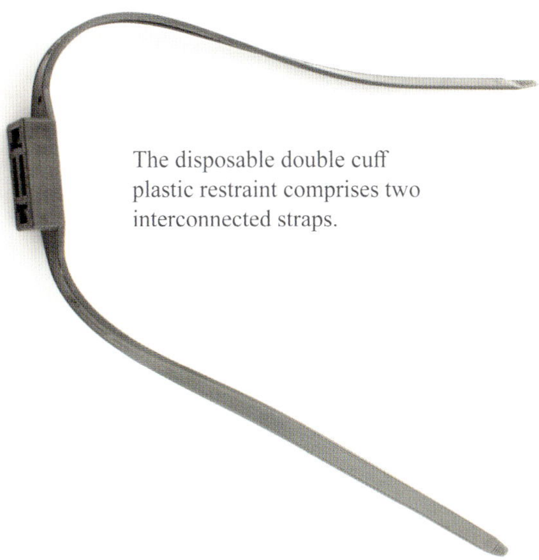

The disposable double cuff plastic restraint comprises two interconnected straps.

These plastic handcuffs are tightened around a detainee's wrists.

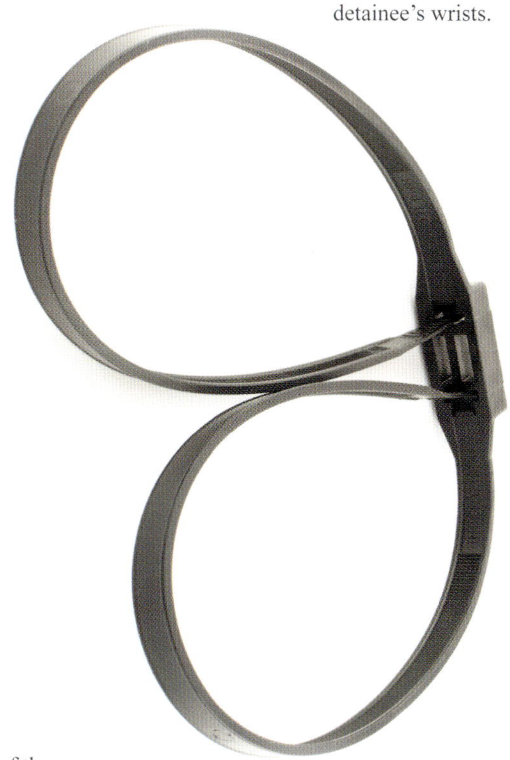

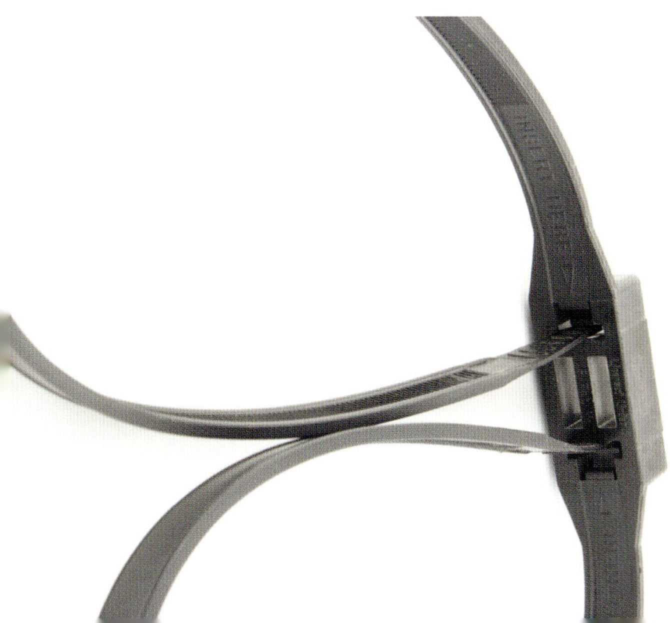

Close-up photo of the tooth lock on a disposable double cuff plastic restraint (detail).

Streamlight Sidewinder tactical flashlight with an articulating head
It has four Lighting Sources: IR LED, White LED, Red LED and Blue LED.

The rotating button initiates a high intensity strobe of the selected light source. The push-button switch in the middle of the rotating button enables and disables the selected light source, starting at low intensity and progressing to the brightest intensity

Streamlight Sidewinder Tactical Flashlight
The large knob at the bottom seals the battery compartment, which holds two AA size batteries.

Helmet mount installed on the MICH for the Streamlight Sidewinder flashlight.

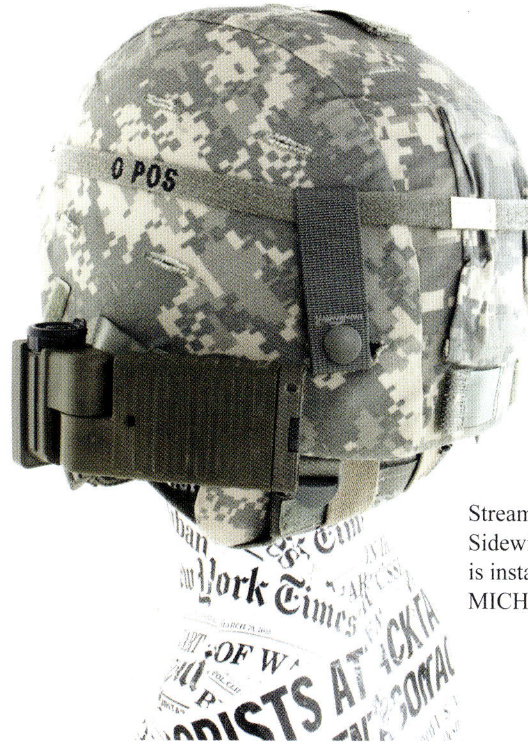

Streamlight Sidewinder flashlight is installed on the MICH (side view).

Streamlight Sidewinder flashlight is installed on the MICH (overhead view).

15. Civilian Contractor on a Training Mission, Instructing Afghan National Army (ANA) Personnel

Instructor in civilian clothes, desert sand color Afghanistan logo baseball hat, civilian desert boots, chinos, olive green rigger's belt, blue short sleeve shirt, coyote brown plate carrier, SAPI plate, multi-tool with a pocket clip in the right pocket, Pistol Cal.45 M1911A1 with private–purchase pistol grips in olive green M12 universal military holster and pistol lanyard.

M12 Universal Military Holster Worn with an Underarm Shoulder Harness
The M12 has an ambidextrous design and is equipped with a removable flap so that it may be converted to a shoulder holster with the UM84H underarm shoulder harness. The harness may be attached to the holster in place of the removable flap, which, in turn, carries a Quick-Lock belt fastener. The underarm shoulder harness allows the holsters to be worn with the pistol in a vertical carry position.

Spare mag pouches are mounted vertically on the right hand-side webbing suspender.

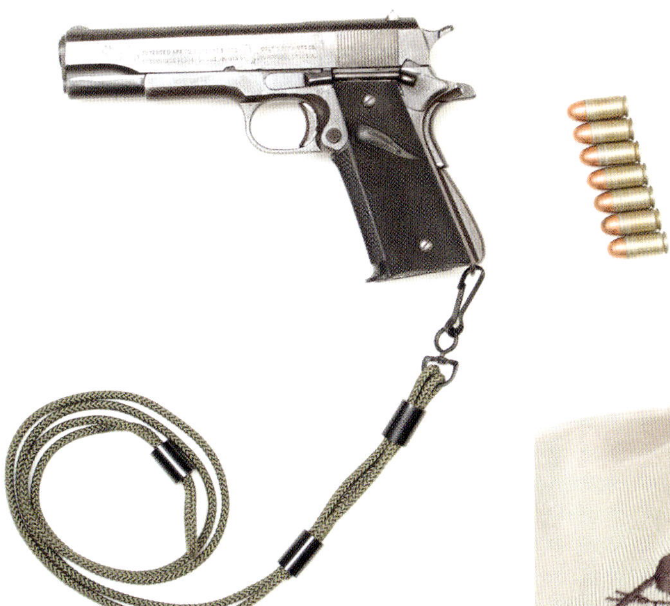

Automatic Pistol, Caliber .45, M1911A1 with private–purchase pistol grips, full wrap-around design, made from rubber with a checkered surface to provide enhanced gripping comfort and controllability.

Desert sand color Afghanistan logo baseball hat.

Hearing Protector Worn Over the Afghanistan Logo Baseball Cap
The ear muffs provide excellent ear protection on the firing range.

The ear muffs have soft, foam-filled ear cushions with excellent sealing properties.

In the extremely high-noise environment at a shooting range they are quite comfortable even in the scorching summer heat in Afghanistan.

Private–purchase tactical desert boots with side zippers for quick donning and perfect fit (side view).

Private–purchase tactical desert boots with side zippers for quick donning and perfect fit (overhead view).

These boots were highly prized prestige items among civilian contractors in 2011 when I arrived and I started a new assignment in Pul-e Khumri, Baghlan Province, Afghanistan. I felt such a strong urge "to keep up with the Joneses" that I bought the first pair for $150 in the PX on the day of my arrival.

They turned out to be absolutely super. Even on rough rocky terrain they make you feel like walking on a set of shock absorbers. Two weeks later they were on sale. I bought another pair for half that price.

The first pair served me well on a long field assignment where I wore them to extinction. Nevertheless, I kept them and I brought them back as souvenirs. I still use the second pair.

If these old boots had an odometer calibrated in light years, it would have reached its maximum reading and it would have rolled over several times! I tied a knot on each shoe lace at half length between the first pair of eyelets on the boots to prevent the long replacement shoelaces from shifting gradually in one, or another direction. The knot keeps them in place.

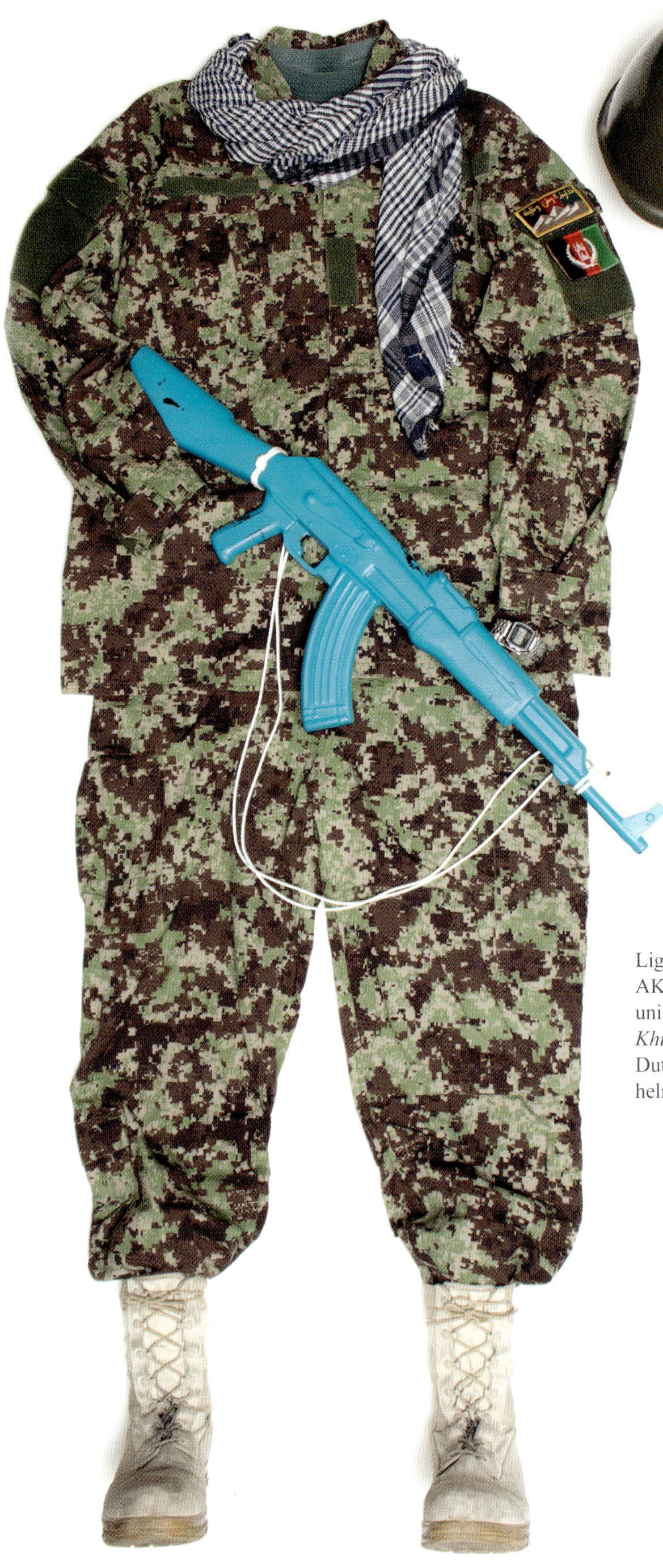

Light blue painted training “rubber duck” AK-47, ANA pixilated digital camouflage uniform, ANA shoulder sleeve insignia *Khudawand-Watan-Wazifa* (GOD, Country, Duty) and national flag patch, Polish wz.67 helmet, *shemagh*, locally-made desert boots.

"Dry practice" for an ANA trainee soldier wearing a Rumanian M73 helmet and the ANA camouflage uniform. Trainees practice gun handling procedures with "rubber duck" AK-47s. The Afghan National Army forest digital camo pattern comprises black, brown, grass green as well as a lighter shade of olive green pixels.

Due to an alarming increase in the frequency of "green on blue" attacks, recruits participating in weapons training sessions were issued hard rubber replica weapons, which were painted in bright, eye-catching colors for easy identification. Some trainees were issued either deactivated real weapons, or unserviceable, defective weapons painted just like the hard rubber replicas.
On one specific occasion I observed young ANA soldiers in a parade unit with vintage Soviet-made Mosin Nagant rifles on their shoulders. The bolt was missing from each rifle.

Shoulder Sleeve Insignia
The overwhelming majority of ANA troops wear the *Khudawand-Watan-Wazifa* (GOD, Country, Duty) Velcro backed patch in conjunction with the national flag patch on their right sleeve pocket. Both patches have been observed in combination with different unit and military specialty patches both on the left and on the right sleeve.

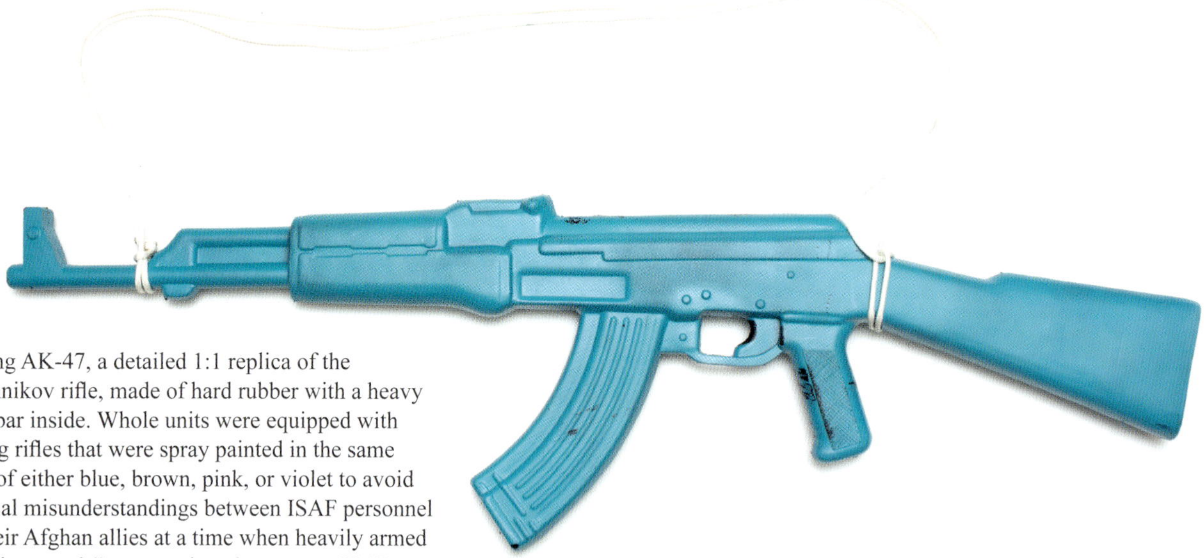

Training AK-47, a detailed 1:1 replica of the Kalashnikov rifle, made of hard rubber with a heavy metal bar inside. Whole units were equipped with training rifles that were spray painted in the same shade of either blue, brown, pink, or violet to avoid potential misunderstandings between ISAF personnel and their Afghan allies at a time when heavily armed "guardian angels" were assigned to protect ISAF military and civilian contract personnel against rogue killers among their Afghan trainees. Some of these mock guns had the fire selector in the "full auto" position, some were made with the selector in the "safe" position. A few had fitted bayonets made of the same hard rubber material, most rifles had no bayonet. Some mock rifles had real sling swivels, most were used for training with a length of parachute cord tightened around the barrel and the butt stock, like this one.

Light blue painted "rubber duck" AK-47, presented together with a real gun for comparison. The real AK-47 is a Hungarian-made weapon with a Chinese sling attached. It is presented exactly in the same configuration as it was last used by an insurgent in 2007 near Bay Saqal, Baghlan Province, Afghanistan.

Manufacturer's label in the ANA coat.
Neck section (detail).

This is my own ANA uniform in size "Extra Large—Long." I received it from my fellow Afghan tarjooman, i.e. interpreter in Pashto, as a farewell present.
Jokingly, he told me that he had to rid an ANA general of his uniform, since only an old general would wear such an enormous size.

Manufacturer's label in the ANA coat.
Inside view, label on the back of the breast pocket (detail).

Rumanian M73 helmet.

While an increasing number of new recruits are issued PASGT Kevlar helmets these days, quite a few ANA troops still wear hand-me-down Rumanian M73 helmets, Polish wz.67 helmets, or old Soviet SSh-40, SSh-60 and SSh-68 helmets.

The chinstrap and the liner of a Rumanian M73 helmet (inside view). The chinstrap on the Rumanian M73 helmet has a double D-ring closure.

Inside view of another Rumanian M73 helmet that I brought back as a souvenir. The Soviet-type four-point chinstrap must be a field modification, the reason for which may remain a mystery till the end of time.

The replacement leather chinstrap is inscribed with the soldier's name, which was *Behroz*, and the number "73" in, what seems to be, white oil paint.

Polish wz.67 Helmet
ANA soldiers were issued a lot of *hand-me-downs* from ISAF contributing nations, including NATO members and non-NATO member countries.

Inside view of a Polish wz.67 helmet.

This Polish wz.67 helmet must have been issued to a long line of Polish conscripts, who left their "graffiti" on the leather liner. In a similar fashion, an Afghan soldier wrote *6374*, assumedly his serial number within his training unit as well as *Sarwar*, i.e. his name on the leather liner.

16. Escort Interpreter Working with the President, Kabul, 2007

K-pot with desert camo cover, SG-1 ballistic glasses, black bullet-proof vest, desert camouflage pattern hydration system carrier, 100% cotton solid brown T-shirt, tri-color desert camouflage uniform: customized DCU coat with additional cargo pockets on both sleeves and DCU trousers with knee pockets for knee protectors.

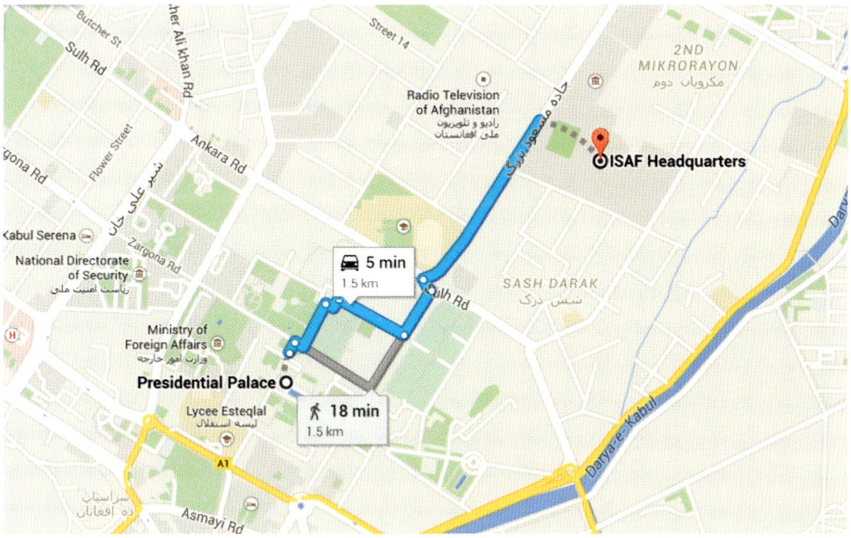

I shot the video en route to the *Gul Khana* Palace on the premises of the *Arg* Presidential Palace compound. On that day, I escorted a visiting politician and I interpreted at his meeting with President Karzai.

These vidcaps come from a short video that I took inside a German Bundeswehr Mercedes Wolf 4WD soon after leaving ISAF Hq, near the intersection of the Bibi Mahrou Road and the Sulh Road in Kabul.

While the delegation was moving around town, I wore my K-pot with a desert camo cover, my SG-1 ballistic glasses, my black bullet-proof vest and a desert camouflage pattern hydration system carrier. I wore a 100% cotton solid brown T-shirt as well as a tri-color desert camouflage uniform with my name tape on the right and a Velcro-back "CONTRACTOR" tape on the left side. I did not wear a "non-combatant patch" with the letters "U.S." on an equilateral triangle, since I was not working on a US contract on that day.

My customized DCU coat had additional cargo pockets on both sleeves. While transferring the breast pockets of one camo jacket to the sleeves of another one seems to be the most common method of customizing a "Coat, Desert Camouflage Pattern, Combat," a local tailor in Mazar-e Sharif utilized an—obviously—liberated piece of fabric with the same desert camouflage pattern and he sewed slightly different sleeve pockets of his own design onto my jacket. It cost me $10 including the fabric and the hook and loop fasteners.

Sleeve pocket with Velcro panel on my customized "Coat, Desert Camouflage Pattern, Combat" (detail). I printed my blood type inside each of my helmets and hats as well as on the Velcro panel on the sleeve pocket. My blood group is O (zero) positive.

The same tailor in Camp Marmal, namely the base of ISAF Regional Command North in Mazar-e Sharif, upgraded my DCU trousers and added knee pockets with Velcro closures on them, so that I can insert knee protectors exactly in the same way knee pad inserts are used in ACU trousers. As far as I recall, that cost me another $10, but I had to supply the knee protectors myself. The knee pads come in handy when someone wearing a full set of equipment has to squeeze himself into an MB Wolf through the rear door, or sit in the confined space of the rear seat in a Hummer.

The knife that—luckily—I never had to use in anger. The relatively short blade has a sharp stabbing point and razor sharp cutting edges.

Knee pocket with Velcro closure for the knee protectors (detail).

When I interpreted in the President's office, I declared the knife that I always carry in a concealed scabbard within the right hand side bellowed cargo pocket, just in time to avoid any possible misunderstandings. I checked it in and I reclaimed it after the meeting. Needless to say, I dropped my protective gear in the entrance hall and during the meeting I wore my DCU only.

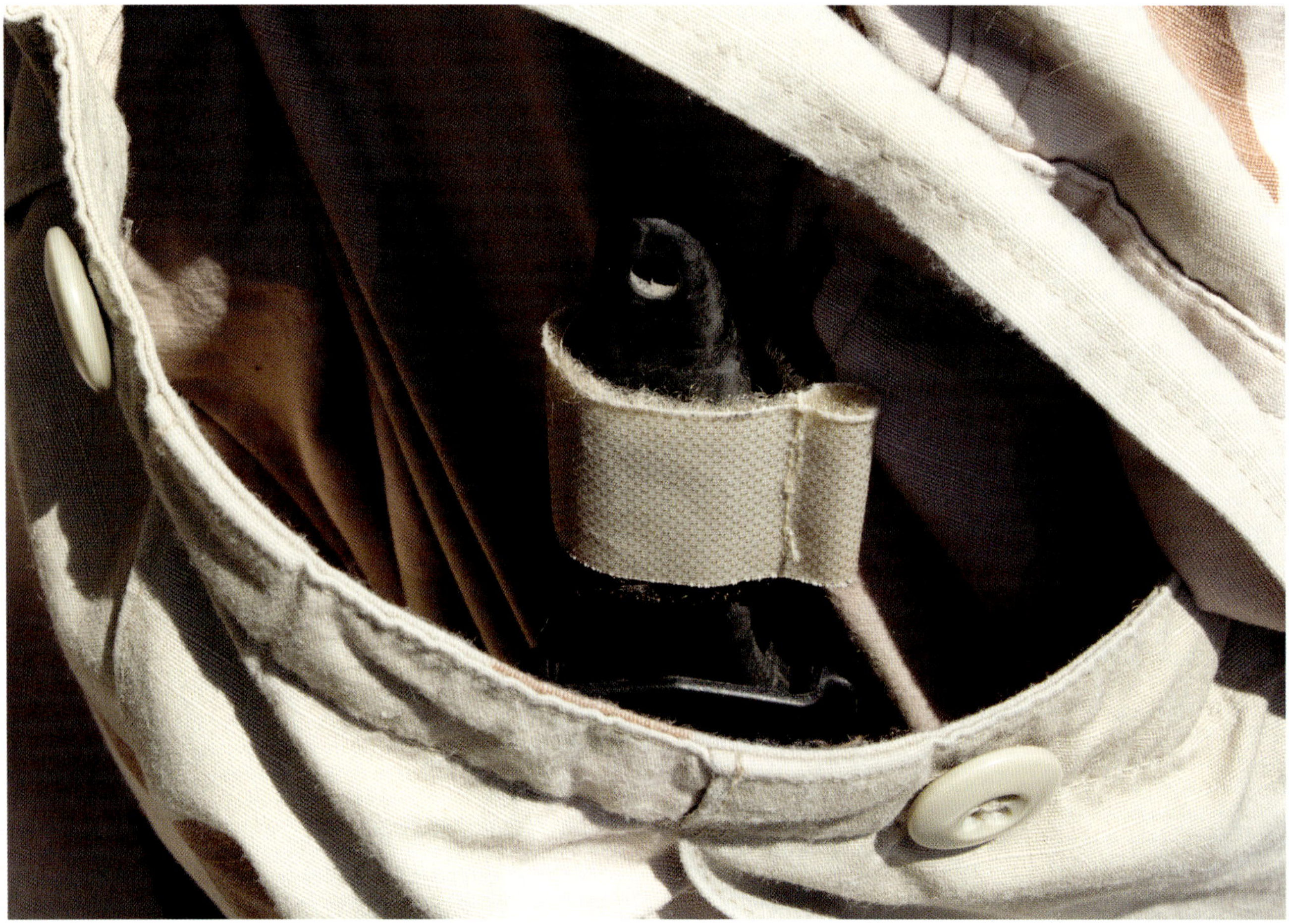

Knife in a concealed scabbard within the right hand side bellowed cargo pocket. The scabbard is stitched to the outer seam on the side of the leg, the grip of the knife is held by custom-made hook and loop fasteners.

Both my client and I received a nice gift from the President as a souvenir. This *Lajaward* (lapis lazuli in Dari) inlay box is handmade and is inlaid with other locally mined semi-precious stones in different shades of brown. It is adorned with the image of the Qala-e-Bost arch. The lapis lazuli inlay box, which came in a matching blue plush-covered gift box, held President Karzai's compliment card. I must admit, I was deeply impressed.

The Arch of Bost

The baked-brick *Qala-e-Bost*, i.e. the Arch of Bost, is approximately eleven miles south of the city of Lashkar Gah, the capital of Helmand province in southern Afghanistan. The eleventh century ruin has been restored recently and it looks quite different now that massive masonry structural supports have been installed under the arch. Nevertheless, it appears on the inlay box, just like on the 1961-series 1,000 Afghani, the 1973-series 10 Afghani, the 1979-series 10,000 Afghani as well as the 2002/2008-series 100 Afghani banknotes in its pristine beauty, exactly in the way it has been adorned by local people, travelers, and conquerors over the past millennium.

17. Escort Interpreter Working with President Karzai, Kabul, 2008

Type A-2 leather flight jacket worn over a private-purchase polyester short sleeve compression T-shirt

I took this cell phone photo of Airport Road about a mile from Kabul International Airport (KAIA) en route to downtown Kabul in December 2008.

I was informed that my client intended to wear his Sunday best at his courtesy call on President Karzai. My client's protocol officer asked me to show up for my interpreting assignment in a suit and a tie, or in some similarly formal attire.

Since I had been working in Afghanistan as a contract instructor for some time and I did not have any formal civilian clothes simply because training Afghan interpreters for the military was supposed to be a field assignment, a Type A-2 leather flight jacket worn over my private-purchase polyester short sleeve compression T-shirt was the most formal outfit that I could come up with on that day.

Type A-2 seal brown goatskin leather flight jacket.

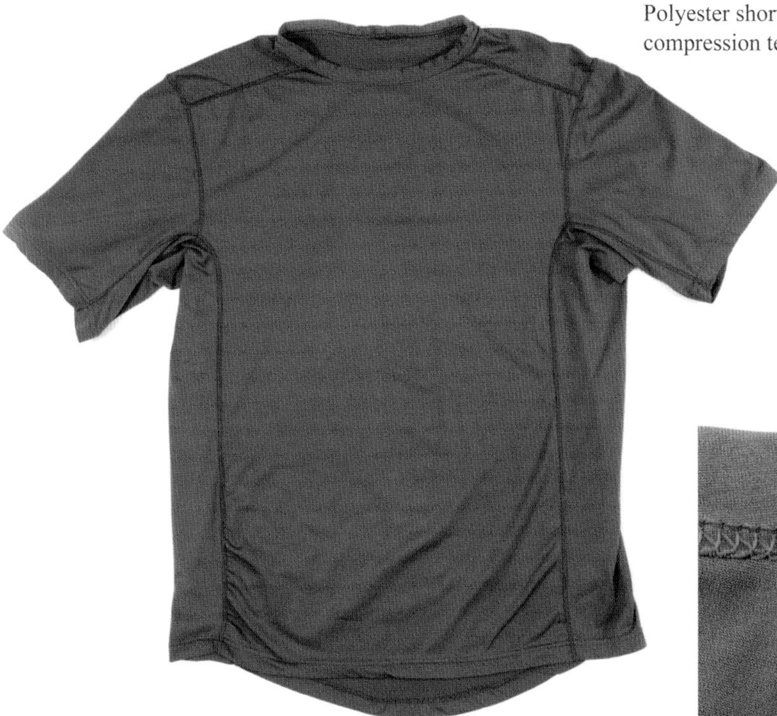

Polyester short sleeve compression tee shirt.

Blackbeard's pirate flag on the label of my T-shirt, which I bought in the Chicken Street Market in Kabul.

Blackbeard's pirate flag on which a skeleton with the horns of the devil is holding an hour glass in the right hand and a spear, or maybe a long arrow in the left hand, while stabbing a bleeding heart must have been designed in the early 1700s to intimidate Blackbeard's victims.

The hour glass was a reminder that time was running out for his victims and the spear pointed at the bleeding heart sent a clear message to naval crews of other vessels that their blood would be drawn and violent death at the hands of the merciless pirates was awaiting them if they refused to surrender. The horns of the devil on the skeleton suggested that the evil and bloodthirsty pirates were in league with the devil himself.

Edward Teach, a.k.a. Blackbeard, was a famous, or rather notorious pirate whose exploits were blown totally out of proportion by modern-day novelists and movie makers. Despite his infamy, he left neither buried treasures, nor a trail of blood behind him. In 1718, he and his ships were hunted down by English vessels along the coastline of North Carolina. Blackbeard was slain along with some of his crew in the ensuing naval battle after Blackbeard's failed boarding attempt against one of the English vessels.

Blackbeard was one out of many colorful characters in the golden age of piracy. Perhaps only Blackbeard himself could tell why his flag was printed three centuries later on the label of a premium quality moisture wicking polyester T-shirt that I purchased in a sealed pack of three for a few US dollars in the Chicken Street Market in Kabul.

Both my client and I received a nice gift from the president as a souvenir. This was the second lapis lazuli inlay box that I received from President Karzai. Also, this one came in a matching blue plush-covered gift box and it held President Karzai's compliment card. I am still the proud owner of this nice souvenir.

This *Lajaward* (lapis lazuli in Dari) inlay box is adorned with a floral pattern. The box is hand made by local artists and the lid is inlaid with Afghan semi-precious stones in different colors.

18. Private Military Contractor in President Karzai's Security Detail, Afghanistan, 2003

Concealable body armor, turtleneck sweater, earphone and voice-activated boom mike connected to a two-way radio in a belt-mounted pouch, angler's vest, 30-round magazines in inside and outside waist pockets, black tactical belt, M9 pistol in cross draw paddle holster, double pistol mag pouch, multitool and desert tan MOLLE radio pouch, M4A1 carbine with one-point bungee sling and tactical light, heavy-duty nylon rigger's belt, chinos, black jungle boots with panama sole.

In the early days, prior to the handover of this sensitive mission to the all-Afghan Presidential Protective Service, for a period of over one year President Karzai's security detail comprised US State Department Bureau of Diplomatic Security special agents as well as private contractors employed and supervised by the Diplomatic Security Service.

The front of the angler's vest is open, the inside and outside waist pockets hold a total of ten 30-round M4/M16 magazines (two in each inside and three in each outside pocket). There is an M9 pistol in a cross draw paddle holster, a double pistol magazine pouch as well as a multitool on the black tactical belt. Also, there is a two-way radio in its belt-mounted desert tan MOLLE radio pouch in the rear (it is not visible in this photo). A heavy-duty nylon rigger's belt supports the chinos.

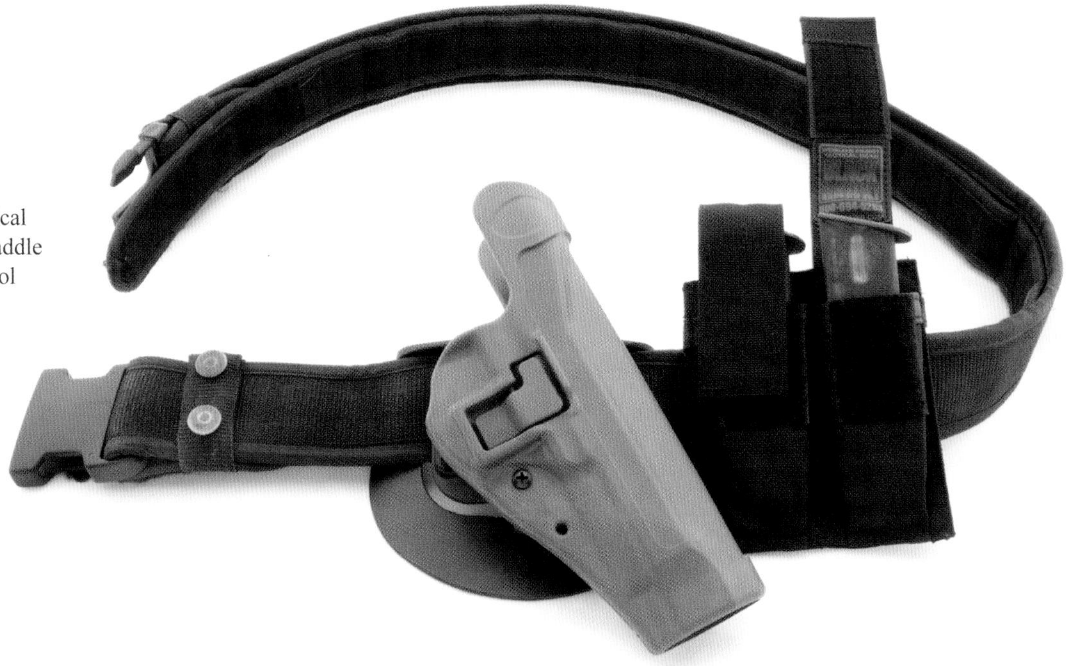

Locally made black tactical belt with a cross draw paddle holster and a double pistol magazine pouch.

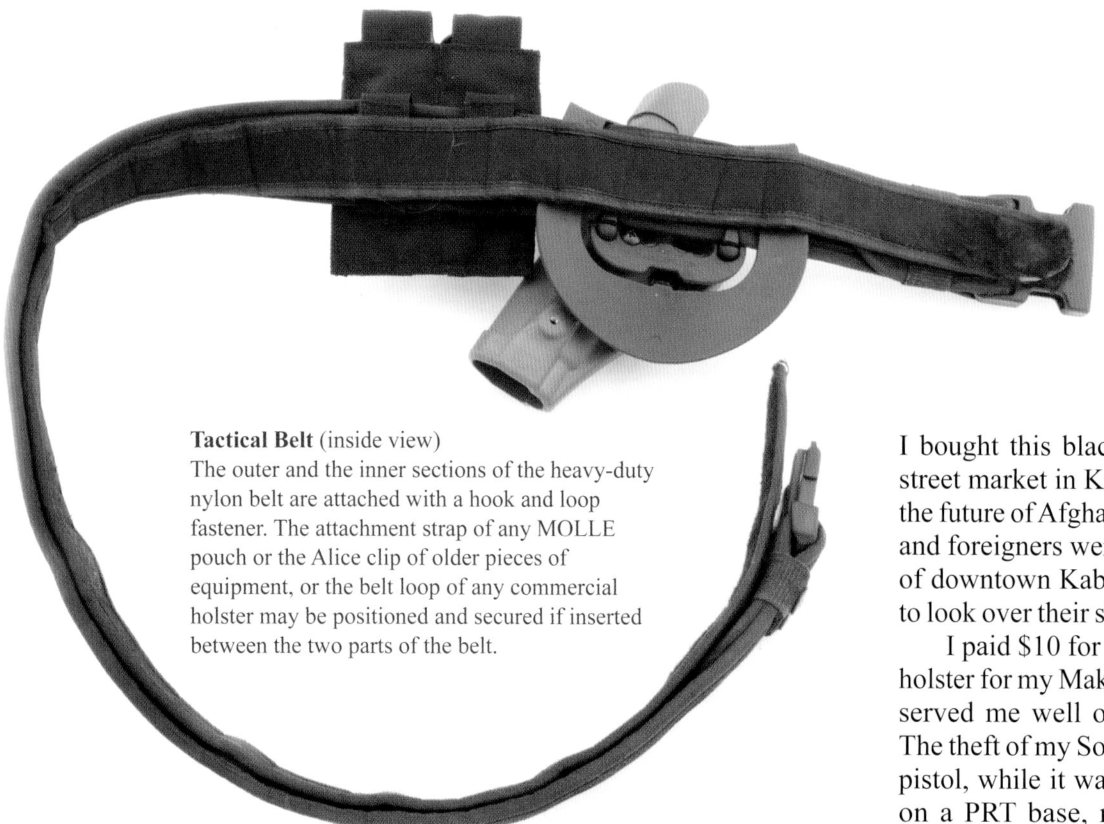

Tactical Belt (inside view)
The outer and the inner sections of the heavy-duty nylon belt are attached with a hook and loop fastener. The attachment strap of any MOLLE pouch or the Alice clip of older pieces of equipment, or the belt loop of any commercial holster may be positioned and secured if inserted between the two parts of the belt.

I bought this black tactical belt in a street market in Kabul at a time when the future of Afghanistan looked bright and foreigners were roving the streets of downtown Kabul without the need to look over their shoulder all the time.

I paid $10 for the belt and a small holster for my Makarov pistol. The belt served me well on many occasions. The theft of my Soviet-made Makarov pistol, while it was in official storage on a PRT base, rendered the small holster useless.

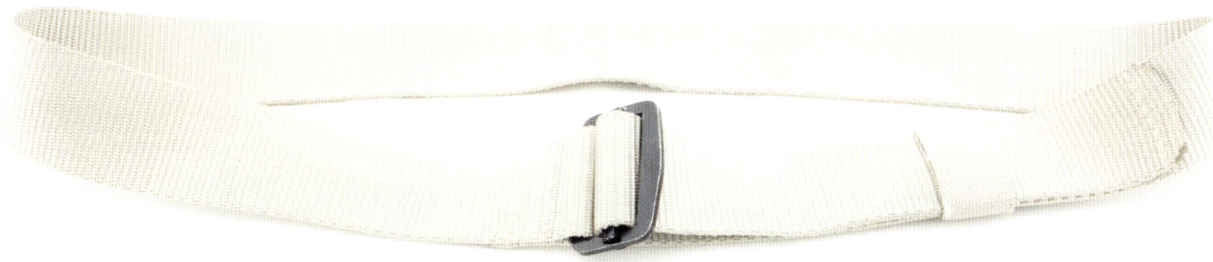

Heavy-duty nylon rigger's belt with a metal friction adapter buckle and an elastic belt keeper.

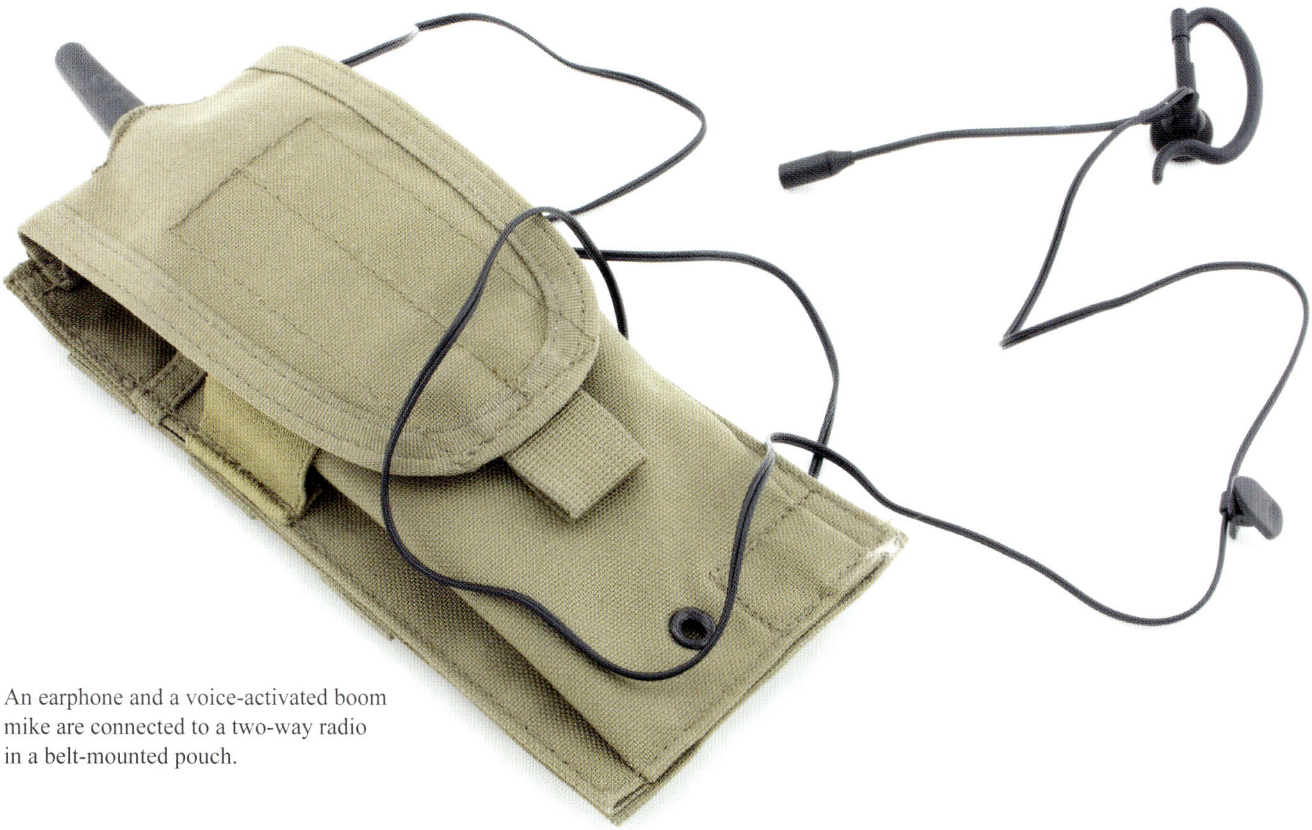

An earphone and a voice-activated boom mike are connected to a two-way radio in a belt-mounted pouch.

19. Special Agent Responsible for President Karzai's Protection in a Private Security Detail, Managed and Supervised by the Diplomatic Security Service, Afghanistan, 2003

Commando recon chest harness, hydration system insulated feed tube held by carabiner, M4 carbine with red dot sight, tactical light and vertical foregrip, three-point sling, M9 pistol in thigh holster, new version of the M9 magazine, mag pouch in desert camouflage pattern attached to the optional MOLLE sleeve on the shoulder strap, two-way radio in belt-mounted desert tan radio pouch (mounted on the rear side, not visible in the picture), acoustic coil tube headset with a push-to talk (PTT) mike and a translucent earbud, the PTT switch is mounted on the Commando recon chest harness, baseball hat, civilian waterproof jacket, foliage green Aramid gloves.

Commando Recon Chest Harness (early model)
On the front MOLLE panel of the chest harness a twin-cell pouch as well as a triple magazine pouch are mounted side by side along with a desert tan first aid pouch. Each magazine cell has a Velcro closure on its lid as well as a grommet for drainage. Each cell can hold two 30-round magazines. The "bib" section of the commando recon chest harness is in the upright position. It could be folded down and stowed in the front plate pocket. The neoprene thermal-insulated hydration bladder tube with a "bite valve" under the plastic valve cover of the hydration system is attached to the bib with a non-locking "D" carabiner (spring clip).

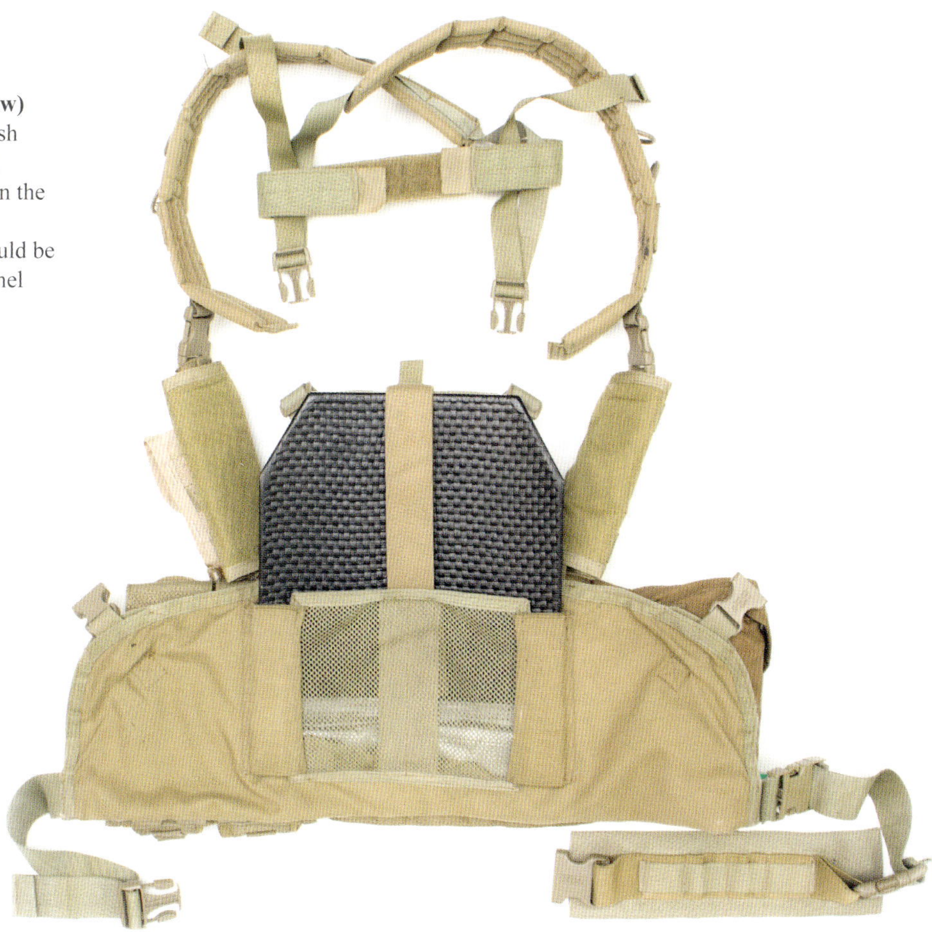

Commando Recon Chest Harness (rear view)
A heavy-duty Trauma Plate is carried in a mesh front plate pocket and is secured by a vertical webbing strap with hook and loop fasteners on the inside of the mesh pocket. The harness has adjustable, padded cross straps. No straps would be necessary, if an optional back plate carrier panel were attached. There are additional MOLLE sleeves on the shoulder straps.

Modified Waist Strap
I had the waist strap on each of my plate carriers and my chest rigs modified either by rearranging the male and female buckles, or by the addition of an extender strap to make sure that I can open and close the waist strap on the front right side instead of the rear side. I admit, the placement of a buckle on the rear side is not a design flaw of the factory-made products. However, buckling and unbuckling a fully-loaded chest harness, or a plate carrier with two trauma plates and additional gear under stressful conditions on the rear right side turned out to be a cumbersome affair for me. It is a matter of taste.

Drop-leg Holster for the M9 Pistol
A set of extender straps with hook and loop fasteners is available to taller persons who like to wear their thigh rig low. The vertical suspender of the thigh rig may be lengthened by a few inches by means of the addition of an extender strap.

M9 magazine pouch in desert camouflage pattern.

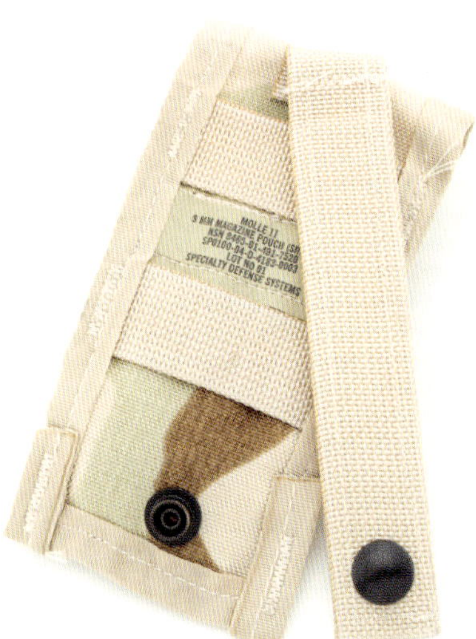

DCU M9 magazine pouch with a new 9 mm pistol magazine.

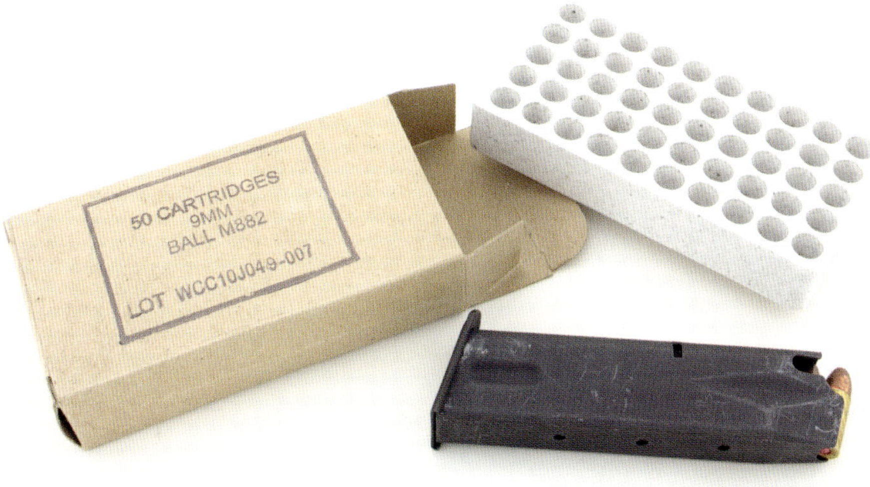

9 mm ammo tray and cardboard box.

The special coating of the latest version of M9 magazines was supposed to prevent the fine sand in Iraq and Afghanistan and dirt from embedding into the surface of the magazines. While I never had any problem with the old ones myself, in about 2008, I acquired a new one just "to keep up with the Joneses." Little did I know that talking about the new ones among colleagues would turn out to be just a fad and replacing old magazines in great haste would be nothing but a fleeting trend.

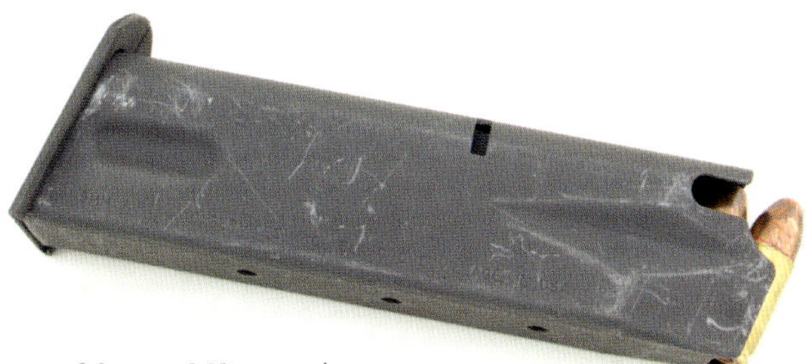

My new M9 magazine.

MOLLE sleeves to be mounted on the shoulder straps with hook and loop fasteners.

20. Special Agent of the All-Afghan Presidential Protective Service

Angler's vest, black body armor with an embroidered patch of the Presidential Protective Service, three-point sling on an M4A1 carbine.

Three-point Sling

The shooter as well as the front and the rear of the weapon are the three points. Hence the name of this sling.

A three-point sling consists of a sling that loops around the upper part of the shooter's body as well as a strap that runs along the barrel, the receiver and the buttstock. This strap is attached to the front sling swivel and the buttstock swivel of the weapon. A highly adaptable three-point sling may be easily positioned as needed, since one end of the sling can slide along the strap. Furthermore, a three-point sling may be converted to a single point sling by sliding a side release buckle to the butt end of the rifle.

Close-up photo of a special agent of the all-Afghan Presidential Protective Service. The buttstock harness of the three-point sling.

The bilingual embroidered patch of the Presidential Protective Service.

While it's not a common sight, this special agent wears the early version of the distinctive bilingual embroidered patch of the Presidential Protective Service on his black bulletproof vest. It is inscribed with *Mahafez Khass Rhays jamhoor*, namely "special presidential protection" in Dari. (*Mahafez*=guard,protective/ *khass*=special/*Rhays jamhoor*= president)

An all-Afghan team of special agents were recruited, security screened and trained under the auspices of the Bureau of Diplomatic Security's Antiterrorism Assistance Program in 2002. The Bureau of Diplomatic Security is the security and law enforcement arm of the US Department of State. The all-Afghan crew members of the Presidential Protective Service were prepared for their personal protection missions and received thorough training from their DS instructors in close protection techniques, security driving, firearms use, land mine avoidance, mass casualty treatment and VIP first aid so that they can take over the close protection duties for the President and the senior leadership in Afghanistan from a private security detail that had been managed and supervised by the Diplomatic Security Service.

21. Afghan Bodyguard of the President

Smart business suit, white shirt and black tie, M68 Close Combat Optic (Aimpoint CompM4) on a Picatinny rail attachment, Grip Pod 02 tactical foregrip with a retractable bipod, M4A1 carbine, 30-round magazines for M16/ M4 assault rifles, 5.56 mm M855 ball ammunition, M856 tracer rounds, spent M995 armor-piercing cartridge cases.

When I first had the honor to escort a visiting guest and to interpret for President Karzai in his office in the *Gul Khana* Palace on the premises of the heavily guarded and completely sealed-off *Arg-e-Shahi* (Citadel of the King) Presidential Palace compound, the gates, the walls, the gardens and individual buildings were guarded mainly by a select group of US State Department Bureau of Diplomatic Security special agents and/or private contractors mainly from the USA.

Visitors were screened, IDs were checked and presents intended for the president, which had to be declared through diplomatic channels in advance, were politely confiscated from visitors by highly-trained and well-disciplined professionals who treated all visitors with a certain measure of contempt.

Next time, in late 2006, I was impressed by a virtually all-Afghan security detail comprising fine young men in smart suits, white shirts and neck ties that made them look solid and conservative. They performed their duties with great sophistication, combined with casual elegance.

Similarly, I was impressed by the high level of professionalism of President Karzai's Afghan security detail when I interpreted for the president during one of his state visits to an ISAF member country.

Roadside posters of Ahmad Shah Massoud and President Karzai outside the city limits, Pul-e Khumri, Baghlan Province.

Picatinny rail attachment to the carrying handle of M16 and M4 carbines. The bolt goes through a whole in the carrying handle and the attachment is secured from below with a large nut.

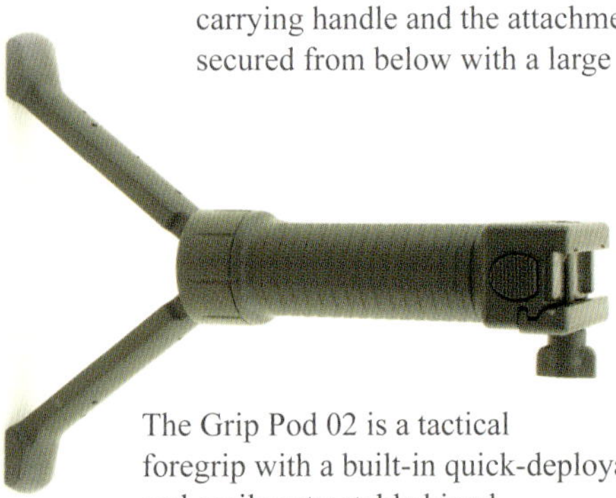

The Grip Pod 02 is a tactical foregrip with a built-in quick-deployable and easily retractable bipod.

M68 Close Combat Optic is the US Army designation of the Aimpoint CompM4 non-magnified red dot aiming device. The Aimpoint gun sight of this Afghan special agent is mounted on a Picatinny rail attachment to the otherwise also detachable carrying handle on the flat-top receiver of the M4A1 carbine.

I bought mine in Kabul. It's not a cheap clone, it's sturdy and it has been used and abused a lot over a period of more than 10 years. However, I am afraid I was ripped off in the street market where I bought it. I guess it is not a genuine military model, since it does not have the manufacturer's markings on it.

After the adoption of the Violent Crime Control and Law Enforcement Act of 1994 in the US, high-capacity magazines were restricted for law enforcement and military use only. Consequently, they were marked accordingly.

Obviously, such restrictions did not apply to civilians (i.e. civilian military contractors) overseas. The Crime Bill expired in 2004, anyway.

30-round Magazines for M16/M4 Assault Rifles
Some are plain and only have the manufacturer's markings on the bottom, some are marked "RESTRICTED LAW ENFORCEMENT/ GOVERNMENT USE ONLY" on the side.

The color and the material of the follower in different mags varied with different series of magazines of different manufacturers.

Green-tipped M855 ball ammunition mixed with orange-tipped M856 tracer rounds in 30-round magazines for M16/M4 assault rifles.

The sequence of different rounds depends on every shooter's individual preference. I would prefer an orange-tipped tracer round to show where the first shot goes. Unless there is any specific reason for a different pattern, I would load my magazines with a 3 x (1 tracer + 3 ball + 1 tracer + 5 ball) combination.

Since the paint on the tips of some of my ammo wore off due to the removal of rounds from magazines and the subsequent reloading of mags many, many times during ANA training sessions, I touched up the green and the orange paint, respectively, with a CD marker pen when I loaded the ammo for myself.

Four-pocket cloth bandoleer holding M855 ball ammunition on 10-round stripper clips. Each carton in individual pockets of the bandoleer holds three stripper clips.

One thing is for sure: the black-tipped AP rounds in these cartridge cases could puncture the engine block of a speeding Toyota and bring the vehicle to a grinding halt in a cloud of Afghan desert sand, dust, and smoke and hot engine oil vapor from an altitude of about 100 yards. The slipstream sucked some spent cartridge cases into the air, but it took only a split second for them to blow back inside the helicopter. Two spent cartridge cases got trapped in folds of the shooter's clothes and were found afterwards.

I quite forgot about them. Miraculously, I found them in the calf storage pocket of my ACU trousers a few years later.

Spent M995 Armor Piercing Cartridge Cases
Two spent cartridge cases of M995 armor piercing rounds. This originally Swedish armor-piercing ammunition was adopted by the US military as the 5.56 mm Armor Piercing (AP) cartridge. The "CG" headstamp belongs to the Nordic Ammunition Company, a.k.a. NAMMO. These M995 rounds were manufactured by NAMMO in 2003. The lines and the dots on the cartridge heads are part of the NAMMO quality assurance and product coding system. According to the manufacturer's specifications these powerful AP rounds can penetrate five inches of hardened steel at 100 meters.

22. On a Wet and Rainy Day: Contractor Wears the Woodland Camo Goretex Parka

Parka, Cold Weather, Camouflage, Woodland camo patrol cap, ACU combat shirt, Inova light, Chinos, black cowhide leather and nylon fabric waterproof duty boots.

Heavy showers and storms followed one another in quick succession for a week in April 2011. Even the surface of compacted gravel driveways and parking areas on the PRT base in Pul-e Khumri, Baghlan Province, Afghanistan became loose and partially flooded.

A Goretex Parka with the matching overtrousers come in handy when all hell breaks loose outside and you would get soaking wet in a split second. Heavy exposure to the elements might as well be as dangerous and damaging to the aramid fiber panels inside an otherwise waterproof fragmentation vest as the immersion of the panels, or the whole vest in water.

Whether water damage can actually lower the resistance of the "bullet-proof" panels to high velocity projectiles or not, I did not intend to find out myself. I protected my own gear as much as it was possible.

Parka, Cold Weather, Camouflage.

Cap, Camouflage Pattern, Woodland Camouflage Printed (front view).

Cap, Camouflage Pattern, Woodland Camouflage Printed (side view).

ACU combat shirt. ISAF identification card and IR reflective blood type patch in a neck ID pouch, dog tag and a small amulet in shrink foil, suspended on a standard bead chain (I placed the other dog tag in my left boot).

Inova Red LED Flashlight
One press of the button activates the high beam, the next press switches on the low intensity light. The third press on the button activates the strobe light operating mode. Squeezing the button for five seconds in the strobe mode activates the signal mode and the flashlight works as a squeeze light.

Inova Red LED Flashlight
A standard embroidered Velcro-back name tag may be threaded through the stainless-steel universal clip and the flashlight may be suspended on the front of a jacket, or a coat. Besides, the clip may be attached to keys, or zippers, or to any other military gear.

MOLLE II, Straps, Lashing
Olive Green as well as Desert tan MOLLE lashing straps.

Olive Green MOLLE II, Straps, Lashing
MOLLE lashing straps were intended for lashing gear to a MOLLE rucksack, or any other pack with MOLLE webbing. However, they are good for a million other purposes. This one doubled up for a trousers' belt on my Goretex overtrousers.

DCU—Goretex jacket
Parka, Cold Weather, Desert Camouflage.

Woodland and Desert Camo—Goretex Overtrousers
The "Trousers, Cold/Wet Weather, Camouflage" and the "Trousers, Extended Wet Weather, Desert Camouflage" are waterproof and breathable overtrousers that keep the legs dry under the worst weather conditions. Even without elastication, or an adjustable drawcord in the waistband of the woodland camo overtrousers, either suspenders attached to the sewn-in loops, or a belt—in this case a MOLLE lashing strap—threaded through the attached belt loops would hold the waterproof overtrousers in place. The DCU Goretex overtrousers have an adjustable elastic drawcord around the waist. The ankle cuffs and the side zips are designed to let the wearer put the overtrousers on, or to take them off without taking his/her boots off.

23. Teacher in an Afghan Girls' School Wears His Desert Tan Aircrew Battledress Uniform, *Tovarish Makarov*

Pakol hat, concealed bulletproof vest, Extreme Cold Weather Clothing System (ECWCS) Level-2 brown-colored turtleneck top and matching drawers, Desert Tan Aircrew Battledress Uniform (ABDU), heavy duty nylon rescue rigger belt, desert tan plate carrier harness with Small Arms Protective Insert (SAPI) ceramic trauma plates, Goretex Desert Combat Boots, ISAF ID neck pouch, Soviet-made Makarov pistol in M12 universal military holster, which is converted into a shoulder holster with the UM84H underarm shoulder harness.

"When Ezmeray pretended to look back, he caught sight of an angel in the distance, walking down the dirt track along the high mud wall of the PRT base and holding his kite out to him. He thought that his tears were messing with his sight, he rubbed his eyes, but *verily, verily*, his kite was still there and the heavenly figure was waving to him. Instinctively, he wanted to run away, but the magnetic force of his lost kite proved irresistible.

What he had thought was a heavenly figure actually turned out to be an old man with white hair and a white beard, wearing sand-colored trousers and a matching jacket. Those in the know would have identified his garment as "Coat, Aircrew, Camouflage Pattern, Combat Tan" made of 95% flame resistant meta-aramid and 5% para-aramid fiber. For a little boy like Ezmeray, not even the shoulder holster with a 9 mm Makarov semi-auto pistol in it and the body-contour fragmentation vest under his service-issue sand-colored T-shirt would have been sufficient proof to the effect that he was a flesh-and-blood human being, a civilian English teacher working in town and not the guardian angel of little kite flyers.

He walked past the outer perimeter security area with a slight limp, he waded through oceans of mud and puddles and he said "*Salaam Bacha*" to him. It is supposed to mean "hello boy." He had a big smile on his face and quite unexpectedly he tussled his thick black hair when he was near him. The pillar of salt named "Ezmeray" slowly transformed itself into a flesh-and-blood *bacha* and reached for his kite. The kite seemed to have levitated into his hands on its own … and the lion cub ran away without saying a single word."

— Excerpts from *Zarbalistan: The Traveler's Ultimate Guide to Ariana*, by Zammis Schein.

DESERT TAN AIRCREW BATTLEDRESS UNIFORM (ABDU)

The desert tan Aircrew Battledress Uniform is made of a flame retardant material. Furthermore, the ABDU offers the added advantage that it looks almost like local clothing from a certain distance. With the addition of local headwear and a *Shemagh* shawl, or a heavy *petoo* blanket in colder weather, it may help its wearer blend into the crowd.

Every day when I went to the other end of scenic Pul-e Khumri, Baghlan Province to teach in my girls' school, I wore a concealed bulletproof vest under my outer garment, frequently the "*Coat, Aircrew, Camouflage Pattern, Combat Tan*." The loose fitting jacket was large enough to hide my 9 mm Makarov semi-auto pistol, which I almost always carried in a shoulder holster.

Carrying a Soviet-made Makarov pistol on a daily basis in town was the logical choice in an environment, where both officers and field agent of the *Amniyat*, i.e. the National Directorate of Security (NDS) on the one hand, and insurgents on the other hand used the same gun and carried the same ammo. In an emergency, when I got stuck in town and when I could not return to the local ISAF PRT base, where I stayed as if I had been a hotel guest, it would have been nearly impossible to buy 9 mm, or .45 caliber ammunition from local dealers, or to capture ammo for an M9 Beretta, or a M1911A1 pistol from fallen enemies. Back in 2011, 9 x 18 mm Makarov ammo was still abundant and almost freely available in rural Afghanistan.

My best friend, *Tovarish Makarov* no. *РГ5686*, a fine 9 mm Soviet service pistol manufactured in 89, was stolen in Pul-e Khumri, Baghlan Province Afghanistan by those, who were supposed to guard and protect me and my gear. Such is life. The '87-dated Makarov in the enclosed photos is a replacement.

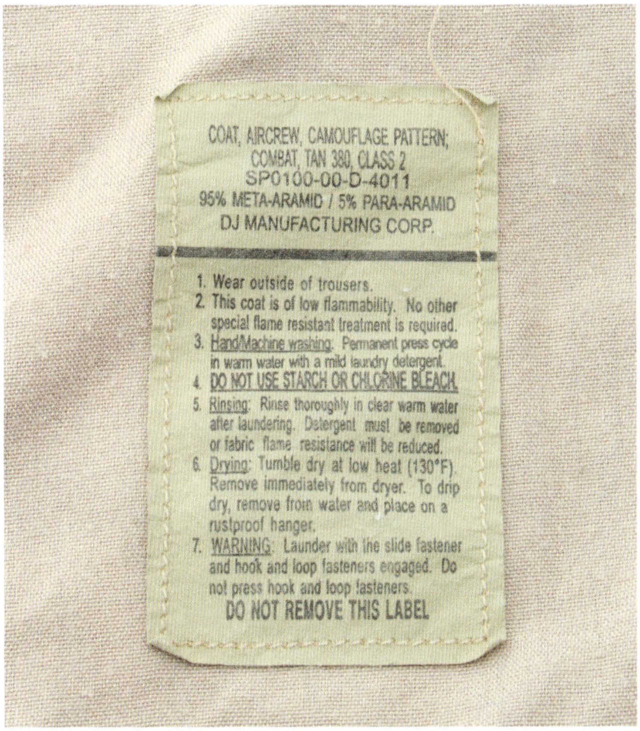

Label in Coat, Aircrew, Camouflage Pattern, Combat Tan.

Trousers, Aircrew, Camouflage Pattern, Combat Tan
The zippered cargo pocket on the left opens from the side, while the thigh pocket on the right has a zipper closure on the top (detail).

Dari-English and Pashto-English dictionaries published by ISAF
Dari and Pashto dictionaries came in handy on a daily basis in spite of the fact that all the Afghan ladies in my women empowerment course were fluent in English.

Coat, Aircrew, Camouflage Pattern, Combat Tan with plate carrier and ID neck pouch (detail).

Field modification of my M12 universal military holster, which is converted into a shoulder holster with the UM84H underarm shoulder harness, to receive my Soviet-made Makarov pistol. The webbing strap around the holster is needed to hold the Makarov, which is smaller than the US service pistols that the holster was originally designed for.

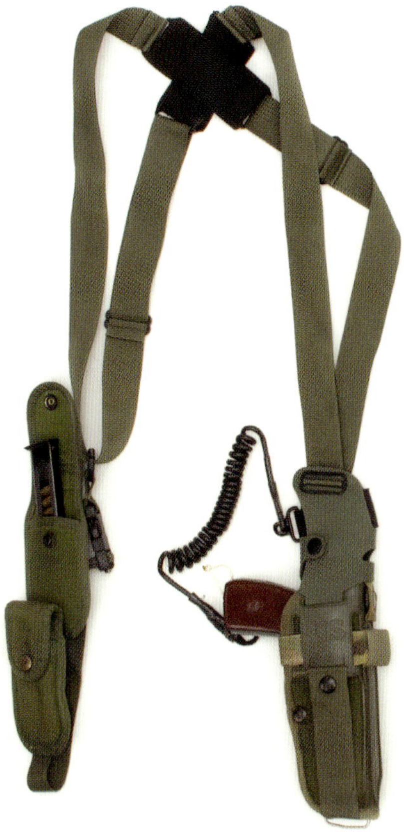

This Makarov is a replacement. It is dated 1987. A nylon rope is attached to the magazine catch just like it was on *Tovarish Makarov*.

"The teacher pulled the short nylon rope on the magazine release catch and the used magazine still with two rounds in it slipped out of the pistol grip. Makarov pistols were notorious for the cumbersome procedure to operate the magazine catch and latter-day gunslingers in Afghanistan who thought that they would ever use the gun in a real combat scenario attached a rope to the catch to pull it fast and easy. He reloaded his pistol in a split second, he flipped the slide catch and the slide traveled forward and picked up the first one of seven rounds of ammo in the newly inserted mag. He learned a clever trick from a local Afghan gunsmith who was a recognized authority on Makarov pistols. He advised the teacher against loading the eighth cartridge in the magazine, because it could compress the magazine spring too hard. The round was chambered instantly and he fired a warning shot into the air. This single shot saved his life."
— Excerpts from *Zarbalistan: The Traveler's Ultimate Guide to Ariana*, by Zammis Schein.

Makarov pistol in M12 universal military holster, which is converted into a shoulder holster with the UM84H underarm shoulder harness. The coiled pistol lanyard, which is attached to the shoulder harness in this case, prevents the loss of a weapon and allows smooth handling of a firearm even in the fully-extended position.

Tovarish Makarov, which served as my self-defense weapon throughout my civilian project in Afghanistan, was photographed on the same Afghan war rug in my room on a PRT base in Afghanistan. This Makarov is a replacement.

My Makarov pistol, serial no. *РГ5686,* which was subsequently stolen from me, rests on an Afghan war rug. I used this small carpet as a background for snapshots I took of my Makarov pistol in my room on the PRT base in Afghanistan a long time ago.

24. Civilian Contract Interpreter, Afghanistan, 2007

Desert camo boonie hat, *shemagh*, SG-1 ballistic sunglasses, multi-pocket utility vest with the client's gold-plated coat of arms, a heavy-duty black bullet-proof vest, brown T-shirt, Korean War vintage US Army M51 trousers, black cowhide leather and nylon fabric waterproof duty boots.

The same outfit without the body armor and the multi-pocket angler's vest. Trousers, Shell, Field M-1951, 100% combed cotton crew neck, short sleeve "rat–brown" T-shirt, *Shemagh*, SG-1 ballistic sunglasses, black cowhide leather and nylon fabric waterproof duty boots, Wibram sole.

I am tall and heavy, I wear size XXL, which is not always a big advantage in places like Iraq and Afghanistan. I admit, the loose-fitting baggy "Trousers, Shell, Field M-1951" in these photos appear to be enormous. In actual fact, they are huge … but they are extremely comfortable, even if a pair of ECWCS Level 2 drawers and a pair of flame-resistant long johns are worn under the outer shell.

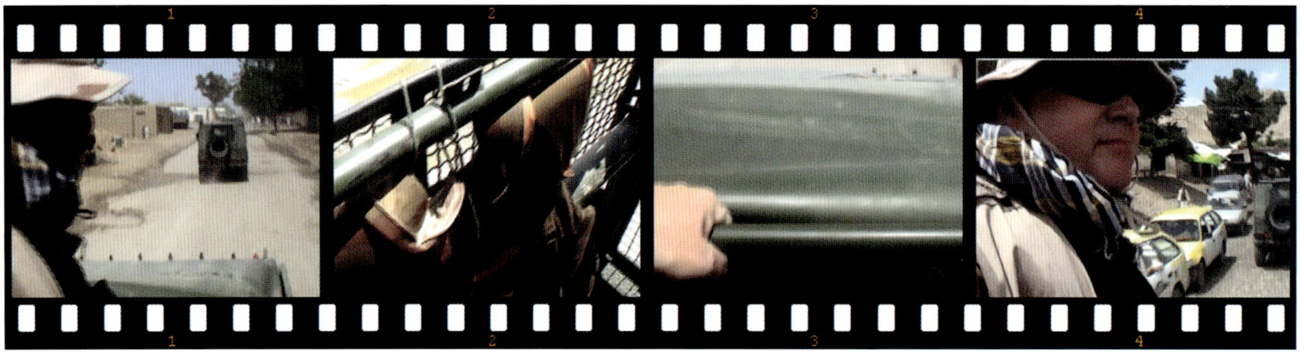

" ... Another Mercedes Wolf at the end of the motorcade carried two soldiers on the front seats, a machine gunner and a civilian contract interpreter in the open rear compartment, which was protected with fragmentation vests slung over the metal tubing."
— Excerpts from *Zarbalistan: The Traveler's Ultimate Guide to Ariana,* by Zammis Schein.

Desert Camo Boonie Hat, SG-1 Ballistic Sunglasses, *Shemagh*
The desert camo boonie hat has an adjustable chin strap and the crown is vented with mesh rivets. "Branch loops," which may hold branches and leaves as camouflage, are sewn around the crown of olive green jungle boonie hats as well the service-issue ACU and the Multi-Cam boonies. However, the branch loops are missing from USGI desert camouflage boonie hats.

Shemagh (detail)

Multi-pocket utility vest, a.k.a. an angler's vest, or a photographer's vest, with the client's gold-plated coat of arms on the right breast pocket flap (detail).

25. "We Do Bad Things to Bad People": Custom Installation of a Tactical Helmet Light on an Afghanistan Logo Baseball Hat

We Do Bad Things to Bad People

On a bright sunny winter day in late 2008, I walked over to the marketplace on the premises of the ISAF Regional Command North base in Mazar-e Sharif to see what kind of local Afghan treasures the licensed Afghan traders had for sale in their small shops on that day.

Also, I checked out the huge chipwood board next to the entrance of the embroidery shop, which advertised a vast selection of patches and inscriptions for which embroidery software was loaded in the state of the art equipment in the workshop behind the store counter.

Instantly, "We Do Bad Things to Bad People" caught my eye. I selected the font type and size as well as the color and I had it embroidered in a curve above the center back opening of my recently purchased Afghanistan logo baseball hat. Whether it was all automatic, or he did it manually, I do not know. I collected my hat with the embroidery on it next morning and I guess I paid $5 for the embroidery.

I myself was on a training mission. I had a lucrative contract to train local Afghan youths to become interpreters for ISAF. Since pretty obviously "I was doing GOOD things to GOOD people," I thought it would be funny to have "we do BAD things to BAD people" embroidered on my cap.

Little did I know that it was the motto of a United States Army Special Forces group also operating in Afghanistan, and that a young prince serving in Afghanistan with British troops virtually in the same time period would make the "We Do Bad Things to Bad People" logo world famous one day.

Custom installation of a tactical helmet light and the matching helmet mount.

The tactical helmet light has three white and two red forward-looking LEDs and a blinking infrared IFF beacon on the side. The light source may be selected with two toggle switches. A pressure switch controls the intensity of the LED light.

Afghanistan logo baseball hat, the tactical helmet light is set to white light.

Afghanistan logo baseball hat, the tactical helmet light is set to red.

I placed a plastic stiffener between the sweatband and the fabric of the hat and I attached the helmet mount with brass nuts and bolts. I attached self-adhesive foam rubber pads to the inner side of the plastic stiffener to make the hat comfortable as well as to keep as much sweat as possible away from the fabric to prevent the sweatband from getting soaked on hot days.

The helmet light may be slid on and locked securely on the matching mount. Also, the lamp may be disengaged by pressing a plastic lever on the mount and by pulling the lamp body off the plastic rail on the mount.

26. Teacher in a Girls' School with His Students Wears His *Shalwar Kameez*, *Whashkaat*, and *Pakol* Hat

Pakol hat, shalwar kameez, whashkaat, concealable "custom made" bulletproof vest, Extreme Cold Weather Clothing System/ECWCS Level1 sand color lightweight top, "anti-exposure" (flame resistant) Aramid fiber underpants worn under the *shalwar*, boot knife, desert boots, Makarov pistol and spare magazines in the inner pockets.

Group photos with a few of my students who were brave enough to pose for photographs with a *khafir*, i.e. an infidel. I wear a pure wool, black *whashkaat*, or waistcoat, over a loose fitting, traditional white *shalwar kameez* outfit, which has the traditional mandarin collar. Both are tailor-made items that gave new meaning to the old advertising slogan "made-to-measure for a perfect fit."

Kids in a local Afghan teacher's class. I supplied some books and teaching aids from my own course budget.

I reached the high watermark in my career when I received a generous grant and I implemented my own women empowerment course methodology in a girls' school that I established in scenic Pul-e Khumri, Baghlan Province, Afghanistan.

The course went very well, but due to the lack of funding and the waning enthusiasm and dedication of my sponsoring organization, the envisaged follow-up course never materialized.

It is weird, but it was the local representative of my sponsoring organization who posed the most formidable challenge to the implementation of my course. I ran into stone walls every time I crossed this person's path.

***Pakol* hat** (side view)
The *Pakol* is a traditional round hat with the sides neatly rolled into a band up to the flat top panel. It is handmade of pure wool. Ribs comprising single, double, or triple rows are sewn in the sides and they serve as an ornament and they give the hat a certain stiffness.

Pakol hat (inside view).

Pakol hat (front view).

Pakol hat (inside view, detail).

I posed at the foot of a billboard where the road forks at the city limits of scenic Pul-e Khumri, Baghlan Province. The road on the left side goes to Mazar-e Sharif, the road to Kunduz is on the right hand side. Ahmad Shah Massoud on the poster wears his *Pakol* hat in the distinctive "Massoud style."

Whashkaat
My *whashkaat,* or waistcoat was made by a tailor in Pul-e Khumri, Baghlan Province in late 2008. While he sewed buttons on the right-hand side, he did not cut buttonholes on the left side, since a traditional waistcoat is not supposed to be buttoned up over the *kameez* shirt.

Whashkaat (inside view)
Two inside pockets have zipper closure and two have buttons. They easily double up as an integral pistol holster, or they can hold a magazine pouch. I carried my Makarov pistol in the zippered pocket on the left hand side and my spare magazines in a twin mag pouch in the inner pocket with a button closure on the opposite side.

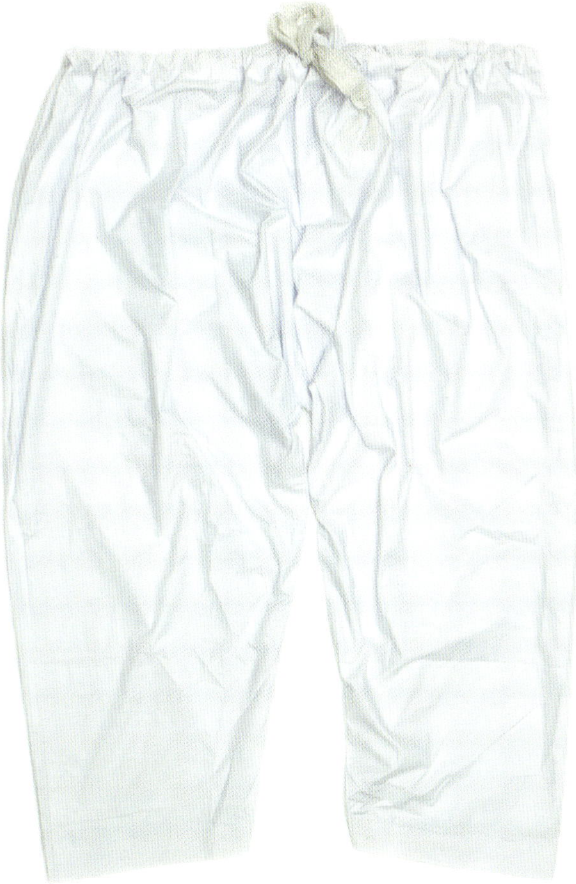

Shalwar, (detail), the loose fitting trousers are tied around the waist with a length of loosely-woven gauze strip.

Kameez, (detail), with the traditional mandarin collar and a side pocket.

Shalwar, leg cuff over my desert boots (detail).

"Anti-Exposure" (flame resistant) aramid fiber underpants were worn under the *shalwar*. As always, I carried a razor sharp boot knife with a flat handle in a similarly flat scabbard (detail).

Extreme Cold Weather Clothing System/ ECWCS Level 1 sand color lightweight top.

ECWCS Level 1 long sleeve lightweight top with thumb holes in the cuffs. The sleeves of the long sleeve lightweight top are longer than usual. There is a slit at the cuff of each sleeve through which the wearer's thumb may be hooked to keep the sleeve in place and to give the wearer's wrist extra warmth and protection from the elements. The cuff may be folded back to reduce the length of the sleeve.

Concealable "Custom Made" Bulletproof Vest
A "liberated" German Bundeswehr fragmentation vest, which I converted into concealable body armor in great haste under compelling circumstances. In the end, I used it for almost nine years.

Concealable "Custom Made" Bulletproof Vest (inside view).

27. Contractor Instructor in CIMIC Convoy to Doshi, Baghlan Province, Afghanistan, 2008

PASGT helmet with "Cover, Helmet, DCU," PT1 glasses, DCU M-65 jacket with oversize green ISAF shoulder sleeve insignia, DCU trousers, ECWCS Level-2 brown turtleneck top and drawers, desert sand color plate carrier with trauma plates, Improved First Aid Kit (IFAK) in a coyote brown pouch, flame resistant coyote brown tactical gloves, desert combat boots, "KEEP DISTANCE" warning sign on Humvee spare wheel.

In late 2008, I had a contract to train local Afghan interpreters for ISAF and I offered on-the-job training to my most talented trainees on field trips and short missions to further improve their skills.

When I resumed my training project after a few days that I had spent on a short and unexpected interpretation assignment in Kabul, I joined one of my trainees when he was assigned to a convoy of three Humvees on a CIMIC mission to Doshi, Baghlan Province, Afghanistan.

I enjoyed a panoramic view of the countryside from the turret of one of the three up-armored Humvees throughout our scenic ride.

I had a chance to wave hello to kids and to shout "*SALAAM*" to some friendly civilians along the road.

Each vehicle in the convoy had an almost identical warning sign on the spare wheel. The sign was a clear indication to any local motorist that if he approaches the convoy and if he gets closer than fifty meters to any vehicle, he would be regarded as a direct threat. The signs were made locally (for further details, see chapter 43).

A host of similar warning signs were mounted on both military and private contractors' vehicles in Iraq as well as on vehicles in US and ISAF convoys on the roads of Afghanistan.

Warnings in Arabic in Iraq as well as Dari and/or Pashto language signs in Afghanistan instructed local motorists not to tailgate these vehicles and to keep a safe distance by all possible means.

Normally, local drivers could be expected to back away when they were close enough to notice a warning sign, even if some of them were illiterate and could not read it at all.

The overall purpose of these signs was to prevent possible suicide attacks. Failure to adhere to a clear warning like this and a million other locally made and often hand-painted signs as well as to approach a vehicle displaying a "keep distance" sign could easily be interpreted as a hostile act and might have resulted in the use of deadly force against local motorists who ventured dangerously close.

Coat, Cold Weather, Field, Desert Camouflage Pattern (DCU M-65 jacket).

Coat, Cold Weather, Field, Desert Camouflage Pattern (DCU M-65 jacket) (detail). The built-in hood can be rolled up and stored in the zippered pouch on the back of the neck.

ISAF shoulder sleeve insignia.

The International Security Assistance Force (ISAF) was the NATO-led security mission in Afghanistan. ISAF was established in late 2001 to train the Afghan National Security Forces (ANSF), to facilitate the reconstruction of Afghanistan as well as to fight the growing (Talib) insurgency against all foreign powers on Afghan soil. The ISAF mission ended in 2014.

The official motto of ISAF was "Assistance and Cooperation," which was printed on the ISAF shoulder sleeve insignia. Initially, the ISAF SSI was circular. Service-issue patches were embroidered on a green background, while quite a few theater-made variants were made in desert sand color. These circular patches, especially the ones with a desert tan background, were also worn by US troops in Operation Enduring Freedom and civilian contractors prior to the appearance of rectangular ISAF patches for the new ACU uniform.

In the final phase of the ISAF mission, the ACU patches of US troops were superseded by rectangular multicam patches along with the gradual replacement of the ACU uniform of almost all combat units in Afghanistan with Operation Enduring Freedom Camouflage Pattern (OCP), namely multicam gear.

All ISAF patches were inscribed with "Assistance and Cooperation," namely the ISAF motto either in Dari i.e. *Kumakh u Hamkahri*, (bottom right patch in desert sand color), or in Pashto i.e. *Kumakh aw Hamkahri* (theater-made oversized green ISAF shoulder sleeve insignia, service-issue green SSI and top right desert tan color patch).

Tactical gloves.

When I was summoned to Kabul for a short interpretation assignment between a visiting government minister and President Karzai, I bought a pair of desert sand color tactical gloves in the PX at KAIA.

I bought the gloves because they are flame resistant, the goatskin leather, which is reinforced in high-wear areas, would last forever and I knew that the injection molded knuckle protector would come in handy when I am thrown around inside an APC, or in the gun turret of a Humvee, for that matter.

Subsequently, when I worked on another contract and I often wore a flame resistant ACU uniform, I bought another pair in foliage green just "to keep up with the Joneses," since all other guys around me wore either identical, or very similar gloves.

I happened to retain my receipt for that purchase in the PX at KAIA.

INSTRUCTOR patch.

Blood Type Patch (my blood type is "zero positive").

Desert sand color plate carrier.

Notices to the local population published in the official ISAF magazine about convoy and checkpoint procedures.

"Every Afghan knew that the official magazine of ISAF was the best fire starter in the whole world and the vicinity of the PRT camp guaranteed a steady supply of weekly editions to the humble inhabitants of Baghlan Province. If there was a way in which the Hungarian PRT actually succeeded in winning the hearts and minds of the local Afghan population, then it was their heroic effort to unleash bundles of ISAF propaganda magazines at members of the local population."
— Excerpts from *Zarbalistan: The Traveler's Ultimate Guide to Ariana*, by Zammis Schein.

28. PSC Operator: "Little Bird" Helicopter Crew Chief/Door Gunner, Baghdad, 2007

Commando chest harness, desert tan first aid pouch with overlapping flaps and Velcro closure, door gunner's safety harness, M4A1 carbine with an Aimpoint Comp M4 red dot aiming device, suspended on a single point bungee sling, M9 pistol in chest rig holster, SG-1 tactical goggles with clear lenses, foliage green tactical gloves, sneakers.

Lightweight Door Gunner's Safety Harness
Safe, comfortable and flexible, worn underneath the chest rig. The gated D-ring and the lift strap on the rear side, over the right shoulder allow unrestricted movement to the door gunner.

This contractor crew chief/door gunner dismounted from his aircraft while he was working on a diplomatic security service detail in Baghdad during Operation Iraqi Freedom. He left his HGU-56/P Rotary Wing Aircrew Helmet with the attached 84/P Maxillofacial Shield on board of the aircraft.

He serves on a highly maneuverable "Little Bird" helicopter, which is painted in a distinctive shade of blue accented with a forward pointing silver arrowhead and a thin white line. Actually, it is a Hughes 369FF model, which was subsequently re-designated by the military as OH-6A Cayuse.

The "Little Bird" under his command provides aerial cover to their principal who travels in convoys on routes in Baghdad that were considered to be the most dangerous roads in the entire universe in those days.

Commando Recon Chest Harness
Two identical triple-magazine pouches are mounted side by side on the front MOLLE panel. The lid of each magazine pocket may be closed with a hook and loop fastener and each pocket has a grommet for drainage.

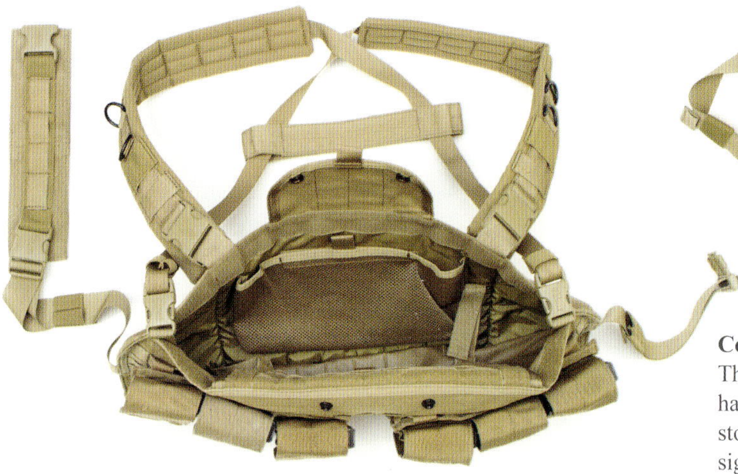

Commando Recon Chest Harness (overhead view)
The "bib" section of the commando recon chest harness may be folded down and may be conveniently stowed in the front plate pocket to achieve a significantly lower profile rig.

Desert tan first aid pouch with overlapping flaps and Velcro closure to hold an enhanced IFAK kit. (attached to the MOLLE panel on the waist strap of the commando chest harness on rear right.) There is a blood type patch on the hook and loop fastener.

The M9 pistol is in a "cross-draw" holster, which is mounted on a chest rig platform on the bib section. For a helicopter door gunner, drawing his pistol in a tactical scenario must be a measure of last resort to save his own life, or to protect his buddies.

Commando Recon Chest Harness (rear view)
The harness has adjustable, padded cross straps. A Small Arms Protection Insert (SAPI plate) is carried in the front plate pocket and is secured by an elastic band in a compartment inside the chest harness.

Chest rig holster for the M9 pistol.

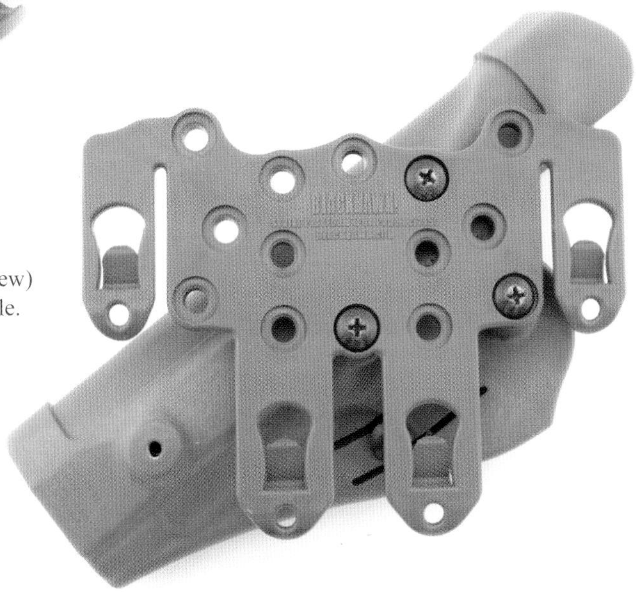

Chest Rig Holster for the M9 Pistol (rear view) The MOLLE adapter platform is clearly visible.

SG-1 tactical goggles with clear lenses.

A single point Bungee Sling absorbs the constant shocks caused by the weapon and it provides exceptional weapon retention.

29. PSC Operator: Door Gunner/Counter Sniper on an MD530 "Little Bird" Helicopter, Baghdad, 2008

Tan aircrew combat pants, tan tanker's (CVC) jacket, *kuffyah* scarf, Vest, Aircrew, Survival, Type I, M9 pistol in thigh holster on right, thigh pad with mag pouches on left, butt stock pouch, M4A1 carbine, M68 AIMPOINT red dot sight, civilian tactical desert boots with side zippers.

This contractor door gunner/counter sniper is a member of the four-man crew of an MD530 "Little Bird" helicopter. The "MD" designation is only due to the acquisition of the original manufacturer by another aerospace company.

When this door gunner flies missions over Baghdad, he keeps his feet on the skids and he hangs out of his door and scans the ground for potential threats.

On the ground he disconnected his vest from the "monkey harness" that tethered him to the aircraft and he dismounted after landing. He left his Rotary Wing Aircrew Helmet behind.

Vest, Aircrew, Survival, Type I
The vest is made from raschel knit and fire resistant Aramid fabrics. The vest has two inside pockets as well as ten outside pockets. All pockets have Velcro closure. A nylon webbing harness system comprising leg and chest straps is permanently sewed to the vest in a cradle fashion. In this way, the vest may be used for tethering a door gunner to the aircraft as well as for a rescue-lift in an emergency situation. The vest has a Velcro-adjustable waist band and a zippered front. A chest harness with a friction adapter secures the vest. Additionally, the vest has front left and right lift attachment loops. The wearer may be tethered to the airframe, or secured to a rescue aircraft in case of an emergency via the lift attachment loops and the gated D-ring on it. The light-weight vest is worn here without the armor plate inserts

Trousers, Aircrew, Combat, Class 2, Tan (detail)
These trousers were made of a flame retardant material.

Combat Vehicle Crewman's Jacket
The desert tan high temperature resistant US military-issue CVC jacket was originally intended for armored vehicle crews. It has rib knit cuffs and a matching knit waist band. The CVC jacket has two front slash pockets with Velcro closure, a zippered pocket with pen slot pockets on the upper left arm as well as a zippered front. Locally purchased *kuffyah*, a traditional scarf

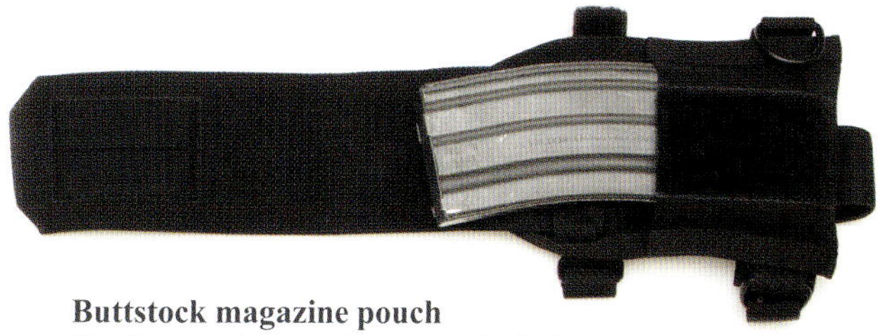

Buttstock magazine pouch
The buttstock magazine pouch is designed to fit the collapsible stock of an M4 carbine, or the fixed stock of an M16 rifle. It holds one spare magazine handy right on the weapon. It has an adjustable hook and loop flap for 20- or 30-round magazines.

Drop-leg mag pouch
The elastic and rubberized leg straps hold the thigh rig secure and make it quite comfortable for the user. Each magazine pocket carries two M4/M16 30-round mags and has a drainage grommet in the bottom. The pouch dividers prevent magazines from clattering.

Drop-leg mag pouch (overhead view).
Buttstock magazine pouch (rear view).

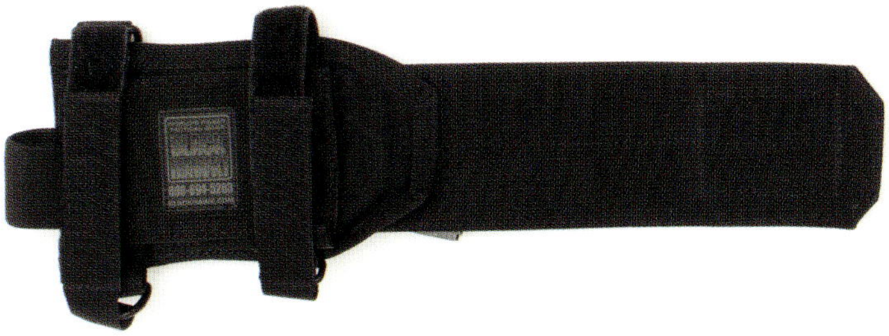

30. PSC Operator: Kurdish Peshmerga PKM Machine Gunner On Board an Up-Armored Escort Truck in Iraq, 2008

Black CVC helmet, olive green balaclava helmet, green tactical goggles, black bulletproof vest worn over an olive green CVC (tanker's) jacket, Army surplus fatigues, black jungle boots with panama soles, and work gloves.

Soviet-made 7.62 mm PKM machine gun and its Stepanov tripod mount on a "DANGER—STAY BACK" bilingual warning sign.

A locally-made "DANGER—STAY BACK" bilingual warning sign, which was intended to be mounted on the tailgate of the up-armored pickup truck (For further details, see chapter 43).

By means of the addition of a Soviet-made 7.62 mm PKM machine gun on its Stepanov tripod mount, which is bolted to the floor, and a ballistically protected gunner's position in the cargo bay, a double-cabin pickup was converted into an up-armored escort truck in Iraq.

The machine gunner in the reinforced housing, which was custom-made of fiberglass sheets sandwiched between heavy gauge steel plates, is a Kurdish *Peshmerga* contractor. *Peshmerga* in Kurdish language means "one who confronts death."

In spite of the fact that Kurds have a long tradition of guerrilla warfare against a host of formidable enemies and that Kurds are considered to be trustworthy colleagues and faithful allies simply because they are not likely to be infiltrated by insurgents, this local contractor is paid less than his western colleagues.

Soviet-made 7.62 mm PKM machine gun and its Stepanov tripod mount, manufacturer's markings (detail).

Black CVC helmet with a "spider-shaped" foam impact liner, balaclava helmet, foliage green tactical goggles.

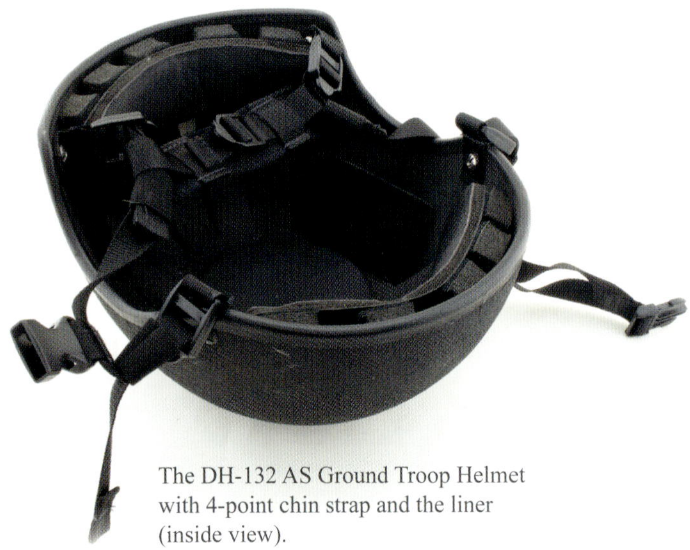

The DH-132 AS Ground Troop Helmet with 4-point chin strap and the liner (inside view).

The DH-132 AS Ground Troop Helmet without the liner (inside view).

Trousers, cold weather, cotton and nylon wind resistant, sateen, olive green army shade 107.

Olive Green CVC (Tanker's) Jacket
The olive green high temperature resistant US military-issue CVC jacket was originally intended for armored vehicle crews. Except for its OG color, it is identical with the desert tan version of this jacket and has rib knit cuffs, a knit waistband, two front slash pockets, a zippered pocket with pen slot pockets on the upper left arm as well as a zippered front.

Green Tactical Goggles
The stealth sleeve has been removed from the goggles and is shifted to the rear. Normally, the stealth sleeve is pulled over the goggles when the goggles are not in use and are stowed on the helmet. The stealth sleeve prevents reflection off the lens and keeps the goggles free of dirt and the lens scratch free.

The "spider-shaped" foam impact liner (detail).

The DH-132 AS Ground Troop Helmet without the liner, the manufacturer's label is clearly visible (detail).

The PKMS 7.62 mm general-purpose machine gun on the Stepanov tripod mount.

The tripod mount is bolted to the floor through the staking holes in each foot of the tripod. The tripod is in the anti-aircraft position and a 100-round ammo can, which holds two 50-round link sections connected with a cartridge between them, is attached to the PKM general purpose machine gun. A 250-round ammo can is held in reserve. The larger ammo can is a local pickup. Since it is unmarked, its origin is untraceable, but it does not bear the raised, embossed star on the side panel.

When the latch for the top cover of the ammo can is pointed downwards and is securely seated in the spring clip on the right leg of the tripod mount, it holds the fully loaded 250-round ammo can in place.

The mounting lugs on either side of the PKM receiver are inserted into the cut-outs in the traverse and elevation mechanism (T&E). In an emergency, the gun with the attached 100-round ammo can, or with the entire length of the non-disintegrating link from the 250-round ammo box, which is mounted on the tripod, may be disconnected from the mount in a split second.

The gunner can easily lift his PKM from the tripod mount and fire it "from the hip" by holding the machine gun by the barrel quick change handle, the pistol grip and the wooden stock. The sling has a shoulder pad to distribute the weight of the gun.

The mounting lugs on the receiver are inserted into the cut-outs in the T&E.

31. PSC Operator in the Last Days of Contracting in Afghanistan, 2010

MICH helmet without a helmet cover, desert tan commando chest harness (early version) with back plate carrier, twin ammo pouches, desert tan IFAK pouch, Pistol, Caliber .45, Automatic, M1911A1 in a "cross-draw" holster, telescopic baton in downward pointing pouch to facilitate quick draw, Inova light, Army Combat Shirt, subdued Afghan flag patch, thigh rig with drop-leg magazine pockets, M4A1 carbine, Grip Pod 2 tactical foregrip with a retractable bipod and a USGI sling. Tilting the gun forward and placing it on the bipod legs and the flash hider next to you is not according to regulations.

Similarly to tens of thousands of his colleagues in late 2010, this contractor can see the writing on the wall. He is filled with a sense of impending doom as the four-month deadline for the implementation of President Karzai's August 2010 decree to disband all private security firms in Afghanistan draws near.

An additional plate carrier back panel is attached to the chest harness to form a full torso rig. The bottom flap has hook and loop fasteners to seal the rear ballistic plate pocket. The waist strap on the right hand side has been modified by means of the replacement of the permanently attached webbing strap on the front panel with a "female" buckle as well as the utilization of the same webbing strap with "male" plastic buckles on both sides. The original arrangement with "female" buckles on the rear panel was too uncomfortable for a bulky person donning the fully-loaded chest harness (inside view of the back panel). A spring hook, or carabiner is locked onto the heavy-duty drag handle and the MOLLE webbing. It may come handy in an emergency. The shoulder strap is threaded into the MOLLE webbing on the back panel for a perfect fit.

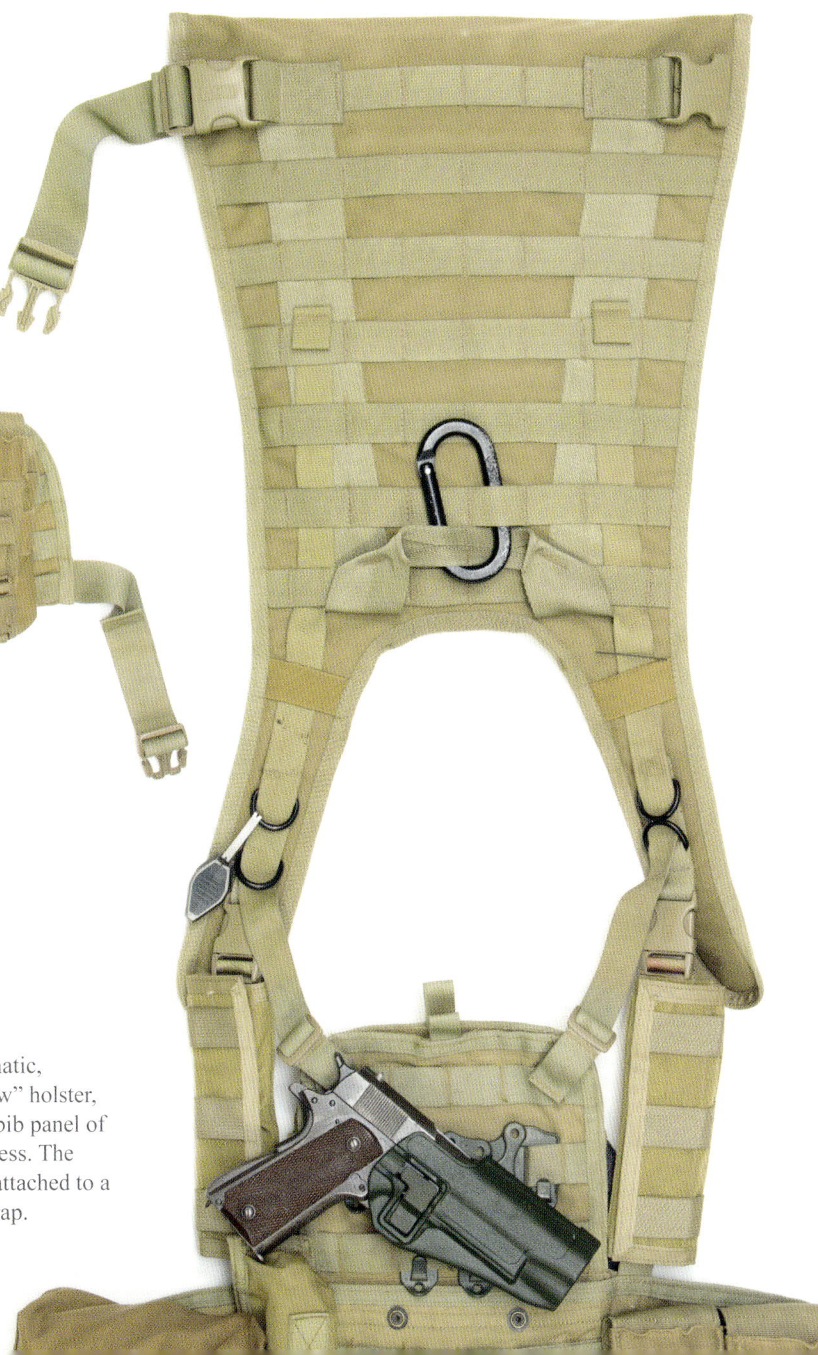

Pistol, Caliber .45, Automatic, M1911A1 in a "cross-draw" holster, which is mounted on the bib panel of the commando chest harness. The INOVA red LED light is attached to a D-ring on the shoulder strap.

Each 30-round magazine is equipped with a plastic loop/magazine assist.

Desert tan commando chest harness (early version) with back plate carrier (rear view). The trauma plate is in the inside mesh pocket and the top of the SAPI plate is held by an elastic band.

Non-locking carabiners (left) and a screw-lock "D" carabiner (right).

Plastic Loop Magazine Assist
The plastic "mag assist" is installed over the base of a magazine and acts as a handle that makes pulling a magazine from its pouch quick and easy. Besides, the plastic loop protects the magazine when it is ejected from the weapon.

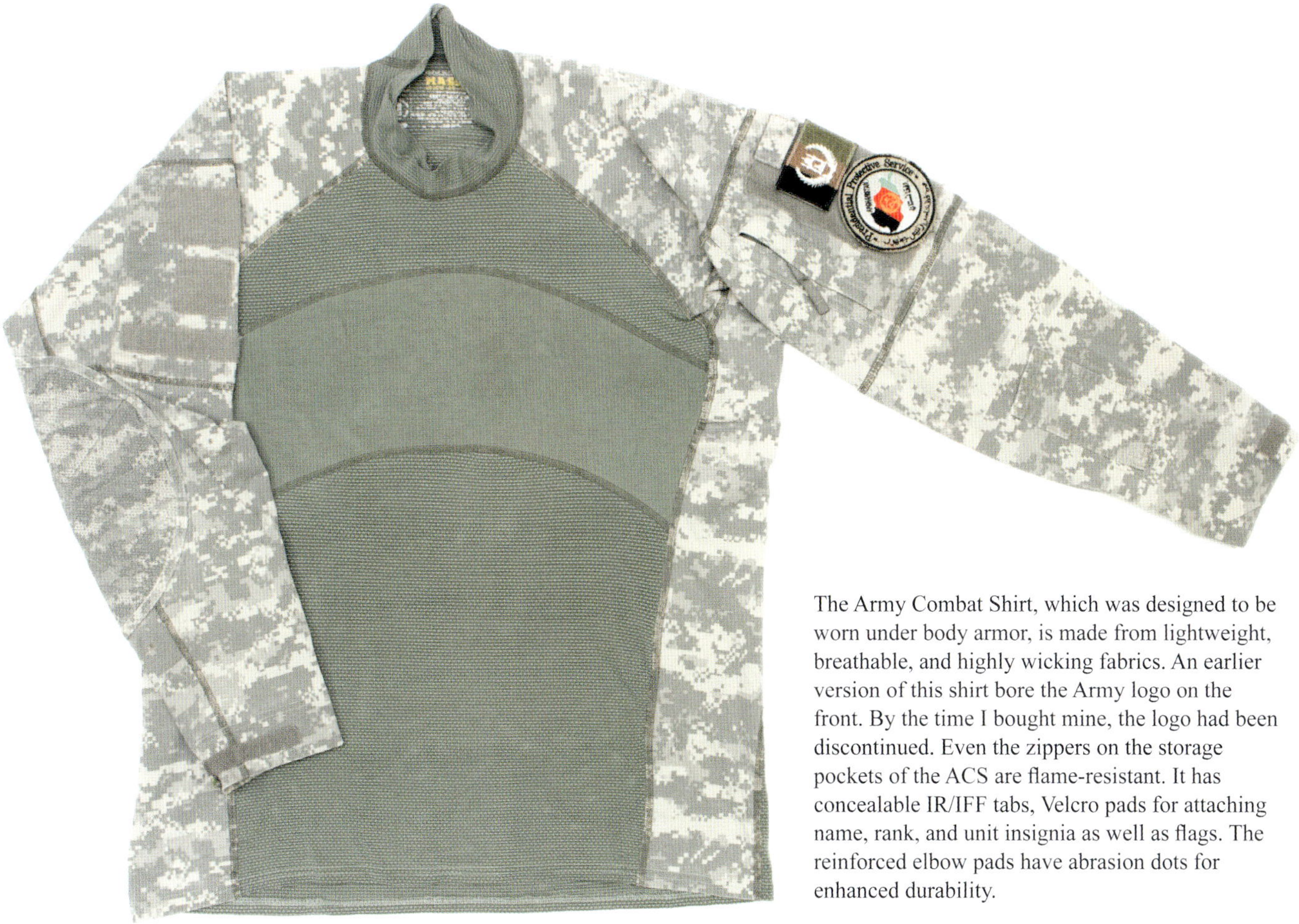

The Army Combat Shirt, which was designed to be worn under body armor, is made from lightweight, breathable, and highly wicking fabrics. An earlier version of this shirt bore the Army logo on the front. By the time I bought mine, the logo had been discontinued. Even the zippers on the storage pockets of the ACS are flame-resistant. It has concealable IR/IFF tabs, Velcro pads for attaching name, rank, and unit insignia as well as flags. The reinforced elbow pads have abrasion dots for enhanced durability.

Subdued Afghan flag, made in an embroidery shop operating on the *Camp Marmal* ISAF base in Mazar-e Sharif, 2010. The *Mehafez Khas Rais Jamhor*, namely the Afghan Presidential Protective Service patch, which is worn under the flag patch on the sleeve pocket, is a memento of an earlier VIP protection assignment in conjunction with Afghan colleagues.

There was a bazaar near the memorial to fallen heroes of the ISAF campaign. The small shops of artisans and traders were arranged in an overturned U shape and additional market stalls were placed in the small square in the middle. In addition to traders who specialized in perfect fakes of looted antique treasures and oriental clones of the latest cell phone models, there were a host of decent merchants who sold precious carpets and fabrics, mementos of the Soviet war as well as genuine Afghan goods. I was a frequent visitor in their stores.

Also, I have fond memories of my short conversations with both embroidery shop owners. This subdued Afghan flag patch comes from one of these workshops.

32. PSC Operator: Member of a VIP Security Detail, Baghdad, Iraq, 2004

Earpiece/mic, collared shirt, white T-shirt, chest rig, INOVA red LED light, chinos, desert boots, M9 pistol in "paddle holster" on right rear (not visible in this photo), M4A1 carbine with a USGI sling.

This contractor is a member of a VIP security detail in Baghdad in early 2004. The dress code for the whole team is smart casual, since each special agent has to maintain a professional appearance in keeping with their principal's status.

Chest Rig and M9 Pistol in a Paddle Holster
(rear view/detail)
The angle of the holster on the paddle is adjusted to the "behind the hip carry" configuration.

Customized waist strap. The permanently attached webbing strap was removed and a female buckle was sewed on the lower right corner of the MOLLE panel. The strap extender has male buckles on both sides and connects the original strap to the front panel. I learned it from my own hard-earned experience that under stressful circumstances this arrangement makes buckling, or unbuckling a fully-loaded chest rig much easier for me.

Chest Rig
Two triple magazine pouches mounted side by side hold a total of twelve magazines. The chest rig has adjustable, padded cross straps. A bib panel is stowed in the internal pocket, which is sealed with a lid and two snap fasteners.

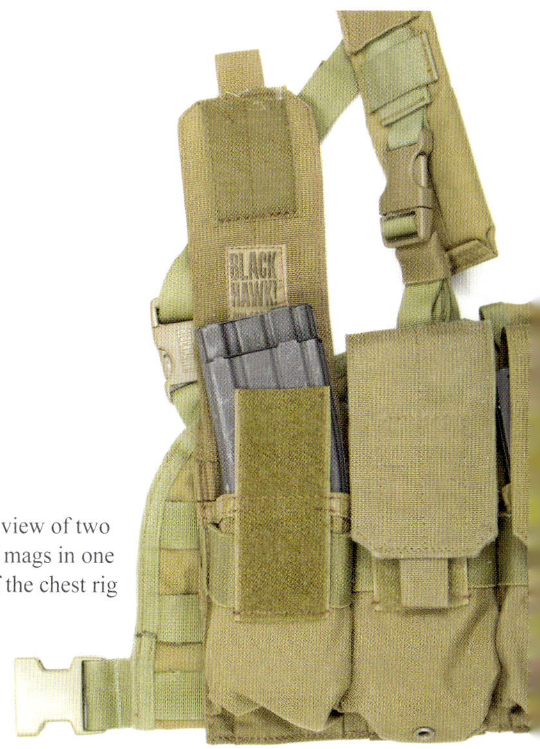

Close up view of two 30-round mags in one pocket of the chest rig (detail).

33. PSC Operator on Convoy Escort Duty, FOB Speicher, Tikrit, Iraq, 2005

Recon chest harness with AK magazines, 1911A1 pistol in the internal chest pouch, DCU radio pouch on a MOLLE shoulder strap attachment, AK-47 assault rifle with IDF sling, work gloves, T-shirt, chinos, desert boots with Panama soles.

This contractor pulled convoy duty in the early phase of Operation Iraqi Freedom. The primary responsibility of his SUV-borne team was to provide convoy security escort between LSA ANACONDA near Baghdad and FOB SPEICHER near Tikrit in Iraq.

Recon chest harness with AK magazines, there is an M1911A1 pistol in the internal chest pouch and a DCU radio pouch is mounted on the MOLLE shoulder strap attachment.

Two-way radio in a desert camouflage pattern MOLLE radio pouch.

1911A1 pistol is tucked into the internal pouch of the chest rig, the securing flap is half open (detail).

AK-47 Assault Rifle With an IDF Sling
The AK-47 in the photograph is a Hungarian-made weapon, which is equipped with an IDF-issue rifle sling.

The same weapon is presented exactly the way it was acquired, namely with a Chinese sling, in chapter 15. Originally, it was collected near Bay Saqal, Baghlan Province, Afghanistan in 2007. This rifle is briefly mentioned in the chapter entitled "Tazi" in *"Zarbalistan: The Traveler's Ultimate Guide to Ariana"* by Zammis Schein.

"One of the Afghans shifted aside his wooden stock AK47 on its newly installed Chinese PLA webbing sling. The Hungarian-made assault rifle was an exact copy of the Soviet-made milled receiver AK47. It used to belong to the soldier who sat next to the driver of the wrecked Mercedes Wolf. The AK got trapped when the 4WD landed on its side and the leather sling had to be slashed with a dagger to cut the weapon loose. With one hand the Afghan guerilla made his prisoner squat and his other hand drew a knife from its leather sheath. From a distance, this looked just like one of the horrific scenes circulating on the internet when terrorists slit the throats of their victims and slaughter them like sheep. There was no time to lose. ... By the time the sniper on the left had acknowledged the order using his throat mike, his spotter said "*Ziel geortet.*" When he identified the man with the knife, he said "*Bereich erhaltet.*" He said "*125 meter*" when he ranged the distance and "*Abfeuern wenn bereit*" when he cleared the gunner. ... The spotter whispered "*Treffer*" when the knifeman's brains and fragments of his skull were splattered all over the mud wall. The other Afghan had one split second to lament the loss of his comrade before he followed him to martyrdom."

Israeli Defense Forces Issue Patrol Sling (detail)
This is the early version of the IDF rifle sling. The original idea was to use paracord loops between the rifle and the reinforced metal clip ends. However, the spring clips could be engaged directly in the AK-47 sling swivels easily. The small "earplug pocket" is suitable for holding a few extra rounds, if the shooter wishes to save the proverbial "last bullet" for himself in case of imminent capture. Pressing the quick release buckle instantly provides a three-inch extension of the sling.

34. PSC Operator on Security Checkpoint Duty Equipped with AKS74U Assault Rifle, Besmaya Military Base, Near Baghdad, Iraq, 2012

AKS74U assault rifle with one-point bungee sling, 45-round magazine in the weapon, a total of six 30-round orange, brown, and plum color magazines in the triple magazine pouch mounted on a desert sand color plate carrier, heavy-duty trauma plates in the front and rear plate carrier panels, two-way radio in the radio pouch on the rear panel, black polyester polar fleece jacket, chinos, desert boots.

Quite a few private security companies, employing a host of private military contractors, remained in Iraq after the withdrawal of the last US troops in 2011. They performed their activities under increasingly difficult circumstances. Their clients, namely the Iraqi authorities, were not very cooperative and raised a number of administrative obstacles. Visas and work permits were not issued, or renewed in time, weapons licenses were not granted, or renewed on schedule, and a number of contractors were apprehended for missing or expired licenses that should have been taken care of by their Iraqi clients. Alas, the Iraqis made their western contractors feel not quite welcome in many different ways.

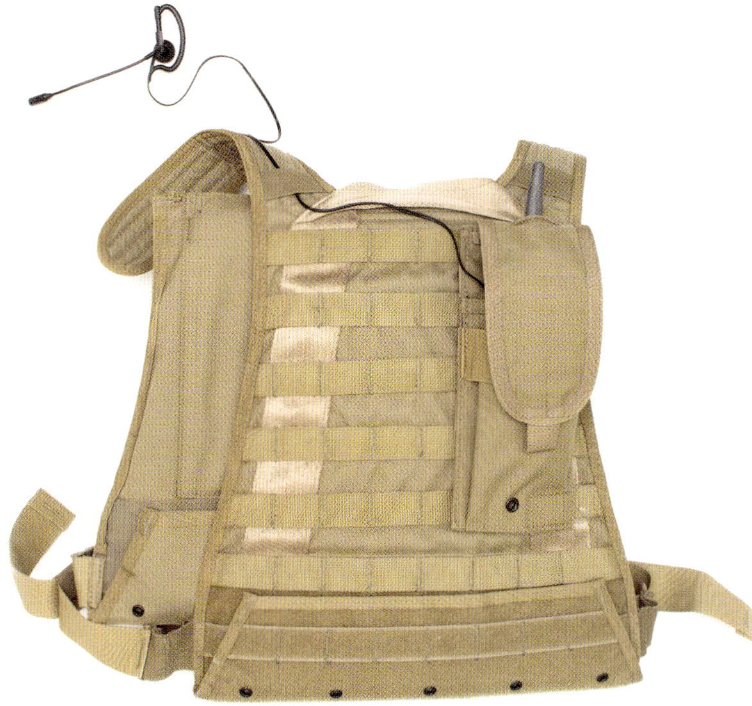

Desert Sand Color Plate Carrier With a Two-way Radio in the Radio Pouch Mounted on the Rear Panel (rear view)
A voice activated boom mike and an earpiece are connected via cable to a two-way radio in a desert sand color radio pouch. The pouch is mounted top right on the rear panel. In this way, it does not interfere with the free movement of the one-point sling on the left shoulder.

Desert sand color plate carrier with a total of six 30-round magazines in the triple magazine pouch.

The butt is folded to the left side (left side view).

AKS74U assault rifle with one-point bungee sling and 45-round magazine in the weapon. The letter "U" stands for *ukorochenneey*, i.e. "shortened" in Russian.

The one-point bungee sling is attached to the rear sling swivel on the folding skeleton butt, the fire selector is in "safe" (right side view).

The skeleton butt is folded out (detail).

Izhevsk-made (marked with upward pointing arrow) and Tula-made (marked with five-pointed star) orange brown and plum color 30-round magazines. The mold number of each mag is on the left side. There are ten 5.45 x 39 mm (training) rounds on a stripper clip with the matching magazine loader attachment mounted on a magazine.

The 45-round magazine, which is 30% longer than its 30-round counterpart, was originally intended for the RPK-74 light machinegun, but it turned out to be very popular with all other AK74 shooters. It bears the MOLOT Arsenal mark on the right side. There is a mold number on the left side (not visible).

35. PSC Operator on Escort Duty Equipped with an AKM Assault Rifle, in the "Green Zone," Baghdad, Iraq, 2006

Commando recon chest harness loaded with AK magazines, CAT tourniquet mounted on the shoulder strap with a Velcro band, tennis shirt, chinos, tactical belt, desert boots with Panama sole, Aramid flight gloves, SPECS sunglasses. He is posing for a photograph next to a SELLING NOT ALLOWED sign outside a shopping bazaar in the Green Zone.

The hard plastic case of the SPECS sunglasses has ALICE clips.

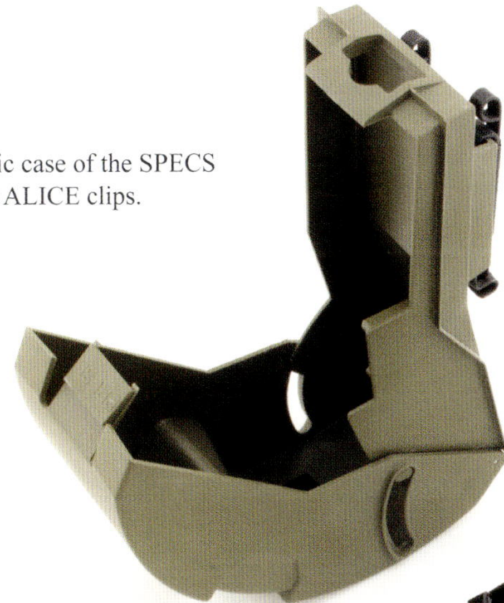

Special Protective Eyewear Cylindrical System (SPECS) sunglasses with a tinted lens (side view).

Commando Recon Chest Harness
Frontal view with open lids, the IFAK kit, the mags as well as the plastic case of the SPECS glasses are visible. There is an INOVA red LED light on the right shoulder strap. The harness has adjustable, padded cross straps and a quick-release waist strap. Similarly to all of my plate carriers and chest rigs, I had the buckle closure moved to the front panel on the right hand side. Four ammo pouches, which can hold two AK-47 magazines each, are mounted side by side on the front MOLLE panel. Each pouch has a lid, which may be closed with hook and loop fasteners as well as a grommet for drainage. The utility pouches on both sides are not wide enough for a full IFAK kit with the tourniquet in the side elastic loop, but they may hold all sorts of useful items, including the hard plastic case of the SPECS sunglasses.

Commando recon chest harness (rear view). The custom arrangement of the buckle closure is clearly visible.

Soviet-made AKM assault rifle, made in the Tula Arsenal in 1971, with original sling and a "bakelite" magazine. A key ring (in some cases a string loop) in the cleaning rod of an AK is a very common sight in Iraq and Afghanistan.

A 30-round steel and a 30-round "bakelite" magazine as well as a 40-round pressed steel magazine are presented for comparison.

The windlass rod and the tourniquet band can be locked with the "C" shaped windlass stop and may be secured with a Velcro strap.

Traumatic combat wounds resulting in significant hemorrhage may be treated with the one-handed combat application tourniquet (CAT). The wounded limb has to be inserted into the loop band, which has to be tightened. Twisting of the windlass rod gradually tightens the tourniquet around the limb and by means of generating circumferential pressure on the wounded limb it stops the bleeding.

36. PSC Operator Wears a Tactical Vest, Arbil (Erbil), Kurdistan, Iraq, 2008

Tactical vest, hydration system with a zippered neoprene insulated hose cover in the interior back pocket, the M4A1 carbine has been detached from the bungee sling, which is still attached to a screw-lock carabiner on the right shoulder, M9 pistol in drop-leg holster.

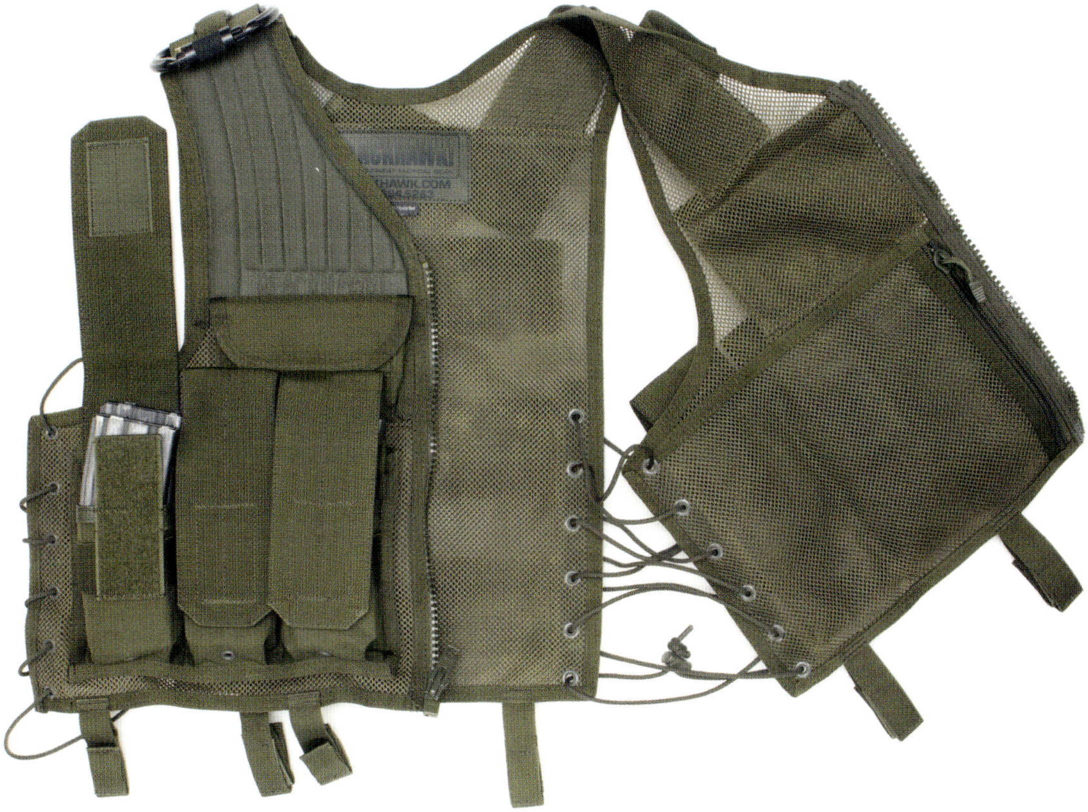

Tactical Vest
The lid is open and there are two magazines in the pouch. The padded recoil pad, the internal zippered accessory pockets and the back pocket as well as the draw strings are clearly visible. The tactical vest has six sewn-in magazine pouches for a total of twelve 30-round magazines on the front and webbing on the back. The vest is made of heavy-duty nylon mesh for maximum breathability and has a padded recoil pad on the right side (this model is intended for right-handed shooters). The size of the vest is adjustable with draw strings on both sides. I've never seen anyone who would have made any practical use of the belt loops along the lower edge of the vest. Theoretically, the belt loops could secure the vest to a web belt. The drag handle on the rear side may come in handy in case of an emergency. The large internal zippered accessory pockets on both front panels may hold a host of useful things.

Insulated Hose Cover
The zipper is open and the bite valve with the on/off switch is clearly visible (detail). The zippered neoprene insulated hose cover for the feed tube of the 3-liter hydration system bladder was available in PX stores. The insulated hose cover keeps the liquid in the tube cool and the bite valve with the on/off switch remains relatively clean and free of sand and dirt.

Single-point Bungee Sling
The elastic-encased "metal all purpose snap hook" (MASH) has large thumb tabs for quick operation. The elastic sleeve is pulled back to display the MASH clip (detail).

37. Civilian Contractor Loadmaster: Humanitarian Airdrop Mission over Afghanistan

Desert Tan CWU-27/P Nomex Flight Suit, AIRSAVE Vest, Green Afghanistan logo hat, combat safety toe flight boots, sage green Nomex flight gloves, combat safety toe flight boots, Humanitarian Daily Ration (HDR).

A civilian contractor loadmaster checks cargo placement before a humanitarian airdrop mission over Afghanistan, during which he will watch thousands of HDR meals on large pallets parachute to the ground.

Aircrew Integrated Recovery Survival Armor Vest and Equipment (AIRSAVE) Vest
The AIRSAVE vest is worn without the optional soft body armor, or hard body armor assemblies. The radio pocket is top right, the general pockets, the pistol holster with an integrated magazine pouch as well as the knife pocket are mounted around the waist. The chest harness with a friction adapter, the front left and right lift attachment loops as well as the leg straps are clearly visible when the zippered front is open. The wearer may be tethered to the airframe, or secured to a rescue aircraft in case of an emergency, via the lift strap and the gated D-ring on it.

Automatic Pistol, Caliber .45, M1911A1 in the pistol holster, spare magazine in the integrated magazine pouch.

Sage green Nomex flight gloves.

Afghanistan Logo Hat
A souvenir from the PX on Bagram Air Base.

Combat safety toe flight boots.

The Humanitarian Daily Ration (HDR) was specifically designed for distribution among the civilian population in crisis areas. The HDR comprises ready-to-eat foods that are permissible for Muslims to eat or drink under Islamic law and which provide an entire day's nutritional requirement. Each HDR ration packet contains two main vegetarian meals and complementary items like bread, a fruit bar, vitamin-enriched biscuits, peanut butter, and spices.

Originally, the packaging was bright yellow for easy identification on the ground when air-dropped for malnourished civilians. However, several aid organizations raised concerns over the alleged similarity between the color of HDR packaging and unexploded BLU-97 bomblets in American cluster bombs, which were air dropped in Afghanistan en masse.

Since local people, especially children in remote areas were not expected to be able to distinguish between rectangular HDR packets and similarly bright yellow, but tubular-shaped unexploded bomblet submunitions lying on the ground, the original yellow packaging was discontinued and subsequently, HDRs were packaged in a salmon-red plastic bag.

38. Civilian Contractor Works as Escort Interpreter, Afghanistan, 2007

Pro-Tec skateboard helmet, SG-1 ballistic sunglasses, black heavy-duty body armor, desert camo hydration system backpack, 9 mm M9 pistol in drop leg holster.

This photo was taken on board of an ISAF transport plane in December 2008, between Kabul and Tarin Kowt, Uruzgan Province.

These snapshots were taken in 2007 while I was working as a civilian contractor escort interpreter and I was traveling with my client, a government minister, from Mazar-e Sharif to Kabul on board of a German helicopter.

I wore my sand-color Pro-Tec skateboard helmet on several assignments in Afghanistan and I loved it. The vent holes on top of the helmet are covered with a fine mesh, which keeps sand, small insects, and foreign objects from entering.

I upgraded the helmet with an aftermarket NVG mount that I bought on the internet. However, I had to realize that night vision goggles on a "rhino mount" would make the plastic helmet too heavy and uncomfortable without a counterweight attached to the rear side of the helmet. If, however, I used a counterweight to keep the helmet with the attached NVG in balance on top of my head, it would make the whole assembly too heavy and bulky for my taste during "kinetic operations."

I mounted a Picatinny tactical rail on the helmet for my helmet cam, or for a flashlight.

Sand-color Pro-Tec classic skateboard helmet and SG1 ballistic sunglasses. The slightly curved Picatinny tactical rail is clearly visible (side view).

Pro-Tec skateboard helmet with rhino NVG mount (front view).

Velcro-back IR reflective combat identification markers in the rear and on the left side. Since the marker patches reflect infrared light when illuminated by a laser aiming device, or they reflect IR light when viewed with an NVG, they help identify friendly personnel in the dark.

Pro-Tec skateboard helmet with a G2 tactical flashlight on the attached rail (side view).

G2 Tactical Flashlight
A flashlight with an extremely powerful beam. It is operated with a pushbutton tailcap, which has to be pressed for momentary-on and twisted for constant-on. The quick-release flashlight mount slides and locks securely on the rail with a finger release lock, while the flashlight is secured in it with a C-clamp (detail).

Two sets of batteries for the flashlight. Service-issue (right) and commercial batteries (left).

Like everyone else who uses a civilian helmet, such as a Pro-Tec skateboard helmet, in conjunction with a tactical communications headset, I had to cut and remove the ear sections of the foam liner on both sides. I lined the semi-circular edge of the foam liner with a Velcro strip.

Although I prefer an acoustic coil tube headset with a lapel-, or sleeve cuff-mounted push-to talk (PTT) mic and a translucent earbud on ordinary days of the week, the noise canceling earphone of any tactical communications headset would require a cutout in the helmet liner.

Pro-Tec Skateboard Helmet (inside view)
Customized foam interior for tactical communications headset kit.

Insulated hose, bite valve, on/off switch (detail).

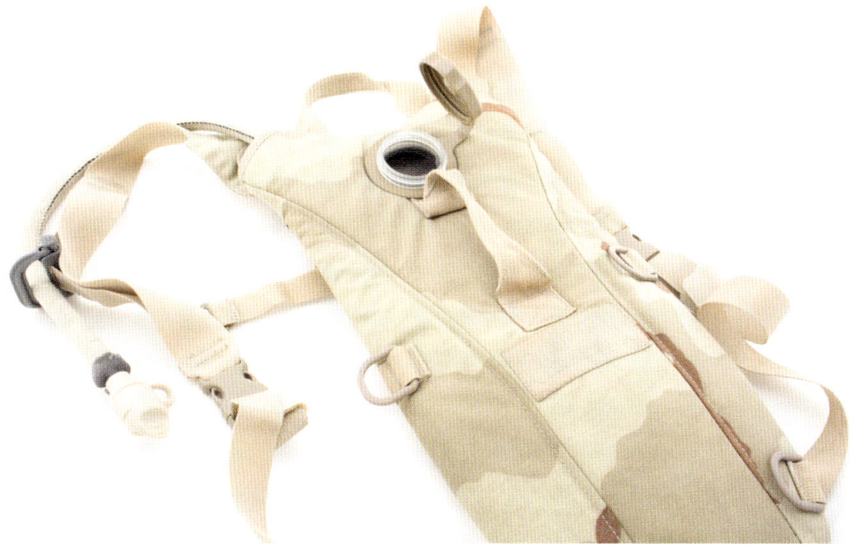

Foliage green GrimLoc spring-loaded locking D-ring on the shoulder harness to keep the insulated hose in place.

3-Liter Desert Camo Hydration System Backpack Mounted on Top of the Flak Vest (rear view)
The hydration system consists of the carrier backpack, the 100 fl.oz. bladder, which is slosh-free and collapses on itself, an insulated hose that keeps liquid in the tube cool as well as a bite valve with an on/off switch. The tethered screw-cap is wide enough for the insertion of a good supply of ice cubes into the bladder on hot days.

39. VIP Escort Assignment, 2007, Afghanistan

Business casual outfit, USA–Afghanistan flag pin, CVC helmet (not visible in this photo) in the coyote brown helmet bag, tactical goggles on helmet-mounted retaining straps, M1911A1 pistol in M7 Shoulder Holster, M1956 pistol magazine pocket, COLT tie pin.

In 2007, the dress code was business casual on a VIP escort assignment in Afghanistan. A jacket and trousers combination with a white shirt and a tie seemed to be more than enough under the prevailing circumstances. I was packing an M1911A1 pistol and I carried two spare magazines in an M1956 "pocket ammo magazine."

Since I was required to keep a low profile, I carried the .45 caliber pistol in a concealed manner throughout my assignment. I made a conscious effort to stay out of public notice and I was determined to keep my CVC helmet in my zippered helmet bag unless all hell breaks loose around me. In this way I could avoid attracting any undue attention to myself. I was just a fly on the wall, while a highly-visible security detail maintained their demonstrative presence in the vicinity of the VIP visitor. An Afghan-US flag pin in my lapel buttonhole and an earpiece with a boom microphone on my left ear was the only tell-tale sign that I was a member of the escort team.

USA–Afghanistan flag pin in my lapel buttonhole. Each member of the team wore a flag pin.

If I had taken my jacket off, my load out on that day would have looked like this.

Black cowhide leather US M7 shoulder holster for the .45 caliber M1911A1.

There is no way to accurately date an M7 holster, since the number stamped into the back side is a drawing number only. All I know for sure is that this US government contractor manufactured and sold M7 holsters to the government between 1982 and the second half of the 1990s and that I bought mine in my favorite Army and Navy store opposite the Port Authority bus terminal on 42nd Street in New York in 2003.

M1956 pistol magazine pocket. The .45 magazine pouch is virtually identical to the M1923 pistol magazine pocket, but in olive drab shade 7. However, it has two metal slide keepers on the reverse for its attachment to a belt.

Colt Tie Clip
A privately purchased gold-plated tie clip for lovers of the automatic pistol, .45 caliber M1911A1.

Converted Combat Vehicle Crewman helmet with tactical goggles in the stealth sleeve (front view).

The Ballistic Liner & Suspension System (BLSS) kit for the PASGT (the Kevlar) helmet was a novelty in those days. The availability of ballistic helmet pads made the conversion of a Combat Vehicle Crewman, a.k.a. a tanker helmet shell into a lightweight tactical helmet possible for the first time. I had a liberated Combat Vehicle Crewman helmet in my war trunk. All I had to do was to remove the padded liner with the integrated headset system as well as to drill two extra holes in the rear section so that I can install the four-point chinstrap from the BLSS kit. I placed self-adhesive Velcro patches that also came with the BLSS kit on the inner surface of the Kevlar shell to hold the ballistic helmet pads in place. A pair of goggle attachment straps were mounted in the rear. Subsequently, I had to install an additional hook and loop fastener in the front to prevent the tactical goggles in the stealth sleeve from sliding upwards. Rubber pads attached inside the left side ear cutout add extra thickness to the helmet shell to support an HL1-A-TN Tactical Helmet Light mount (inside view).

MICH and CVC helmets, flak vest, plate carrier on top of my locker in my room (living container) on a PRT base in Afghanistan.

Converted CVC Helmet (side view)
The low-profile earpiece with a boom microphone is clearly visible. The flexible microphone boom swivels to allow accurate positioning behind the chin straps. This headset is hooked up to a two-way radio and operates in the voice activated mode, which is preferable to a communications system comprised of an earpiece and a lapel-, or cuff-mounted PTT microphone, when both hands have to be free all the time. Actually, full compliance with the communications system of the security detail of my client was mandatory.

CVC Helmet Cover with Elastic Edging
The DCU helmet cover may be attached to the helmet shell via the use of the elastic edging plus the hook tabs. The cover also includes slits for goggle attachment straps in the rear of the cover. I must admit I never mounted the cover, but I always intended to.

CVC helmet with ESS tactical goggles, the stealth sleeve is removed and is held by the elastic strap (side view).

Goggle attachment straps hold the tactical goggles in the stealth sleeve (rear view).

40. Teacher in an Afghan Girls' School Wears the Fishtail Parka, 2011

M-65 fishtail parka, *pakol* hat, *shemag*, heavy-duty cotton duck carpenter pants, black cowhide leather and nylon fabric waterproof duty boots, helmet bag.

Vid caps from a cell phone video about a routine daily taxi ride from my girls' school to the PRT base where I was staying. Pul-e Khumri, Baghlan Province, 2011.

I worked as a teacher in my girls' school and I moved around a lot in downtown Pul-e Khumri, Baghlan Province either in a taxi cab, or on foot. My work was deeply embedded in the local community.

I admit I carry sentimental feelings towards some items of clothing that I wore on specific assignments, or which may remind me of my younger years. However, pure nostalgia is not the only reason why I wore my M-65 fishtail parka on cold winter days in 2011 in Afghanistan.

My size XL overcoat was warm and comfortable. Since it was my outermost garment, the bulky gear that I carried underneath remained hidden from the curious eyes of local people in the street, or in the market.

Most important of all, from a certain distance it resembled a *petoo*, a large heavy shawl that Afghan men wrap around themselves to keep warm while outside during winter. The loose-fitting parka helped me blend into the crowd.

The detachable synthetic fur-trimmed hood of the M-65 fishtail parka.

In the first few days I also wore the detachable synthetic fur-trimmed hood, but I realized that I stuck out like a sore thumb with the white fur wrapped around my neck. From then on, I wore my fishtail parka without the hood.

The M-65 fishtail parka with a removable quilted liner (inside view).

The lower edge of this overcoat is shaped like the tail of a fish so that the coat can be tied around the thighs. Hence the name of the fishtail parka.

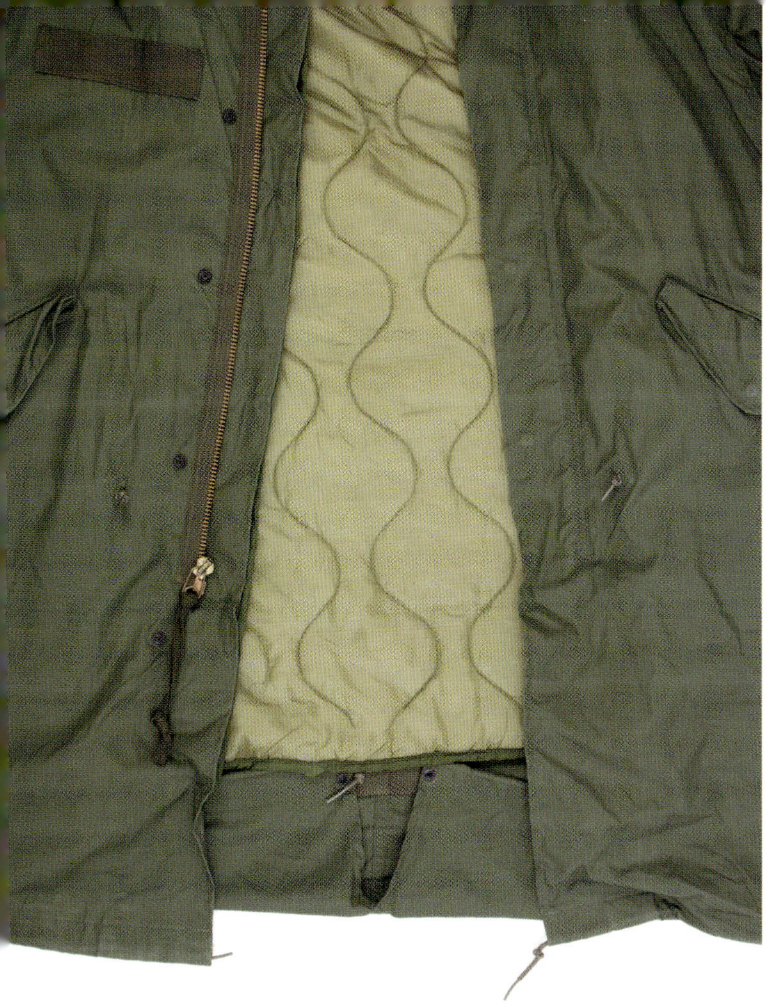

The lower edge of the parka. The fishtail section is folded up and secured with the snap connectors. (inside view, detail). Although the olive green fishtail parka is not waterproof, it can be sealed around the neck and the wrists and the removable quilted liner makes it quite warm when it is worn over other layers of clothing.

Helmet Bags
I used a helmet bag as a carry-all bag. It has two large outside pockets with both Velcro and snap closure. Inside the bag has two smaller pockets. The helmet bag has padded side panels, large carrying handles, a snap hook and a metal zipper. In addition to the service-issue olive green "BAG, FLYER'S, HELMET," coyote brown and black bags were also available in the PX at ISAF HQ in Kabul.

41. Contractor a Few Days before the Evacuation of All US Personnel from Balad Air Force Base, Iraq, June 2014

SG-1 glasses, black vest, two-way radio in black radio pouch (mounted on the left shoulder on the rear side, not visible in the photo), acoustic coil tube headset with a push-to talk (PTT) mike and a translucent earbud, M9 pistol in drop-leg holster on the right-hand side, thigh pad with double mag pouches on the left side, black tactical belt with double pistol magazine pouches and combat casualty response kit in zippered ACU pouch (mounted on the rear side, not visible in the photo), chinos, sage green Corcorans.

AKMS assault rifle with a 75-round drum magazine (overhead view).

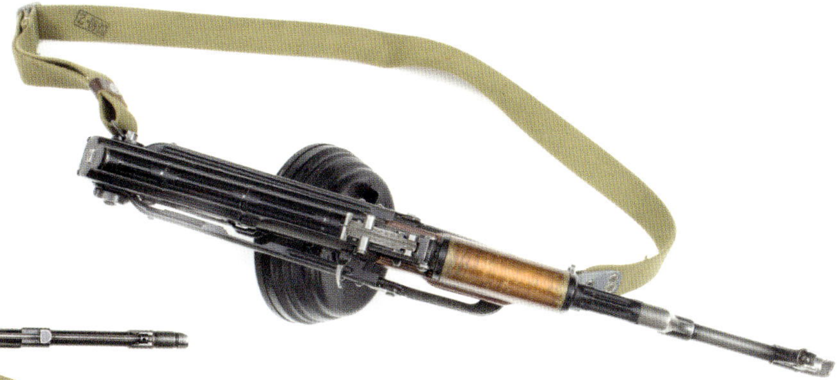

AKMS assault rifle with a 75-round drum magazine (bottom view).

75-round drum magazine, the tower at the top of the drum magazine inserts into the magazine well of the AK rifle (detail).

75-round Drum Magazine
Originally intended for the RPK light machine gun, the AK drum magazine offers significantly increased fire power at the cost of its extremely heavy weight.

Combat casualty response kit in zippered ACU pouch (top view).

Combat casualty response kit in zippered ACU pouch in a thigh rig configuration with a belt loop and a rubberized thigh strap (rear view).

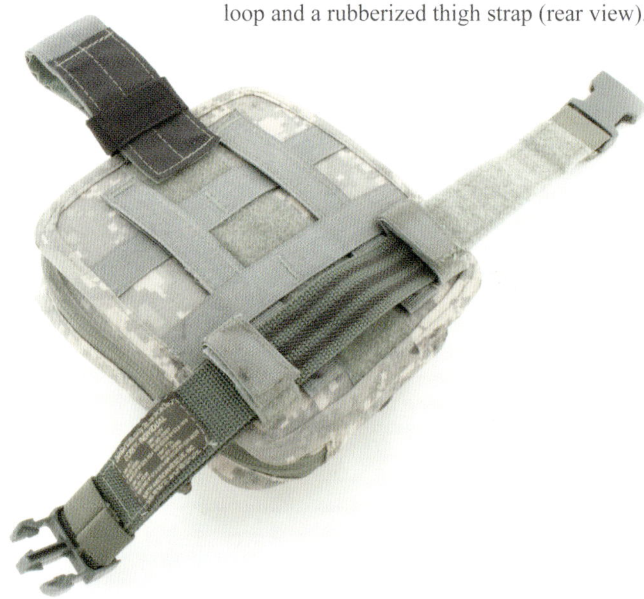

Customized contents of an enhanced combat casualty response kit (detail).

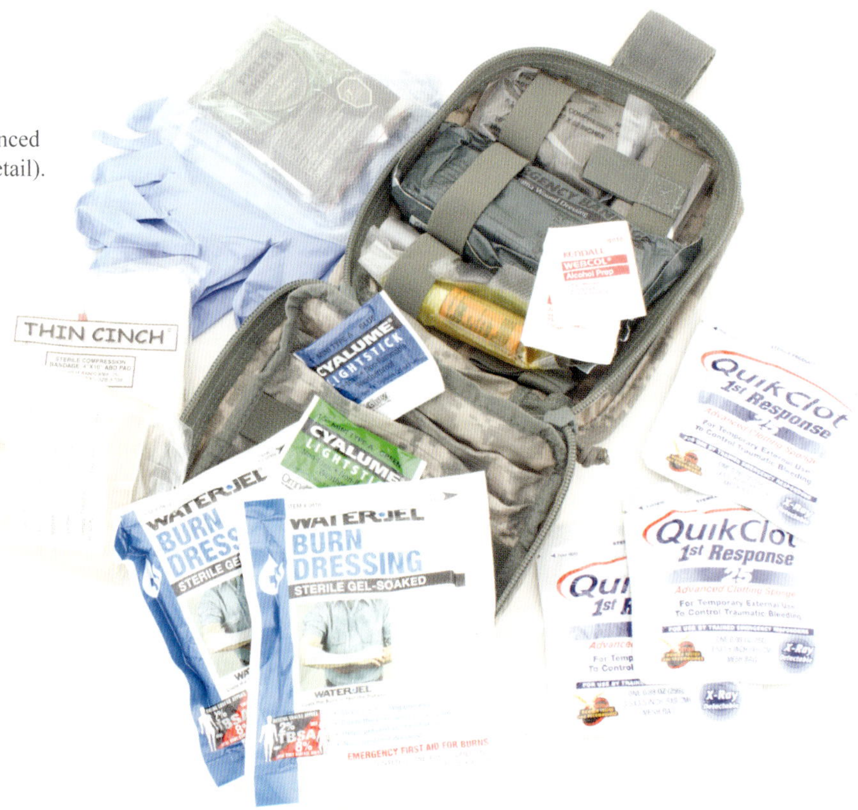

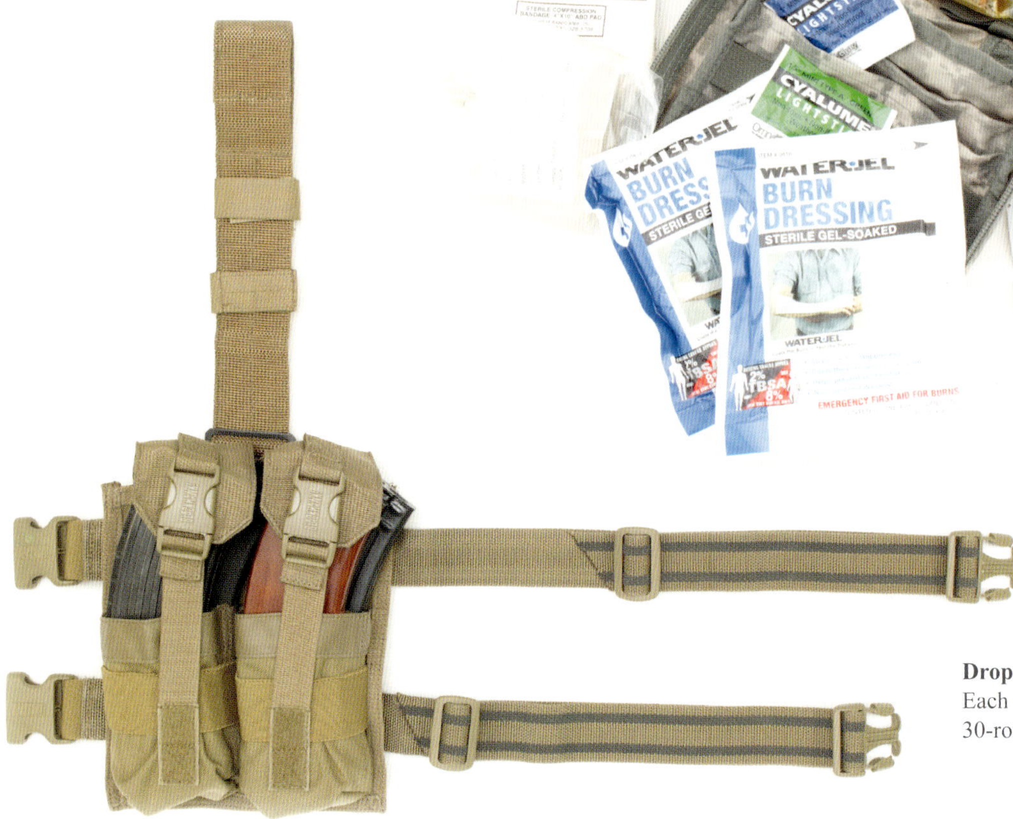

Drop-leg mag pouch
Each magazine pocket carries two 30-round AK magazines.

Two-way radio in black radio pouch, which was mounted on the left shoulder on the rear side, acoustic coil tube headset with a push-to talk (PTT) mike and a translucent earbud.

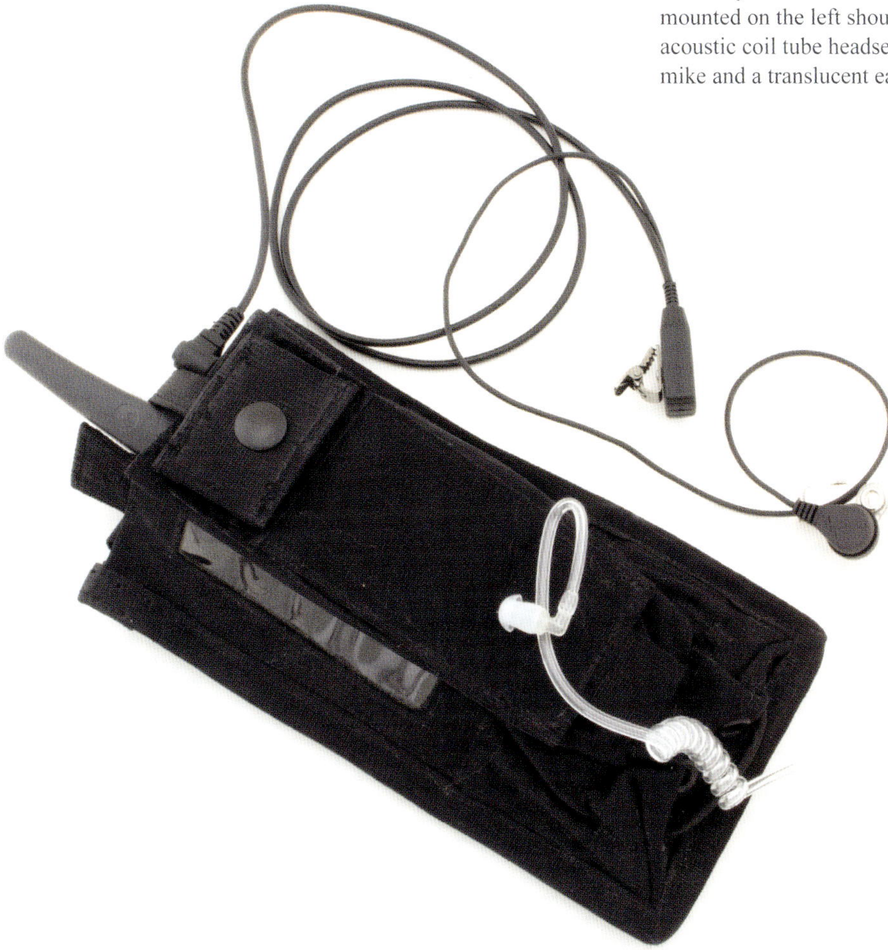

Sage green Corcoran boots.

42. Deployment and Redeployment

Luggage Tags on a Chartered Flight
The NATO air-bridge linked a few European military and civilian airports with Termez in Uzbekistan, where the former Soviet airfield could handle the heaviest transport aircraft as well as with several airfields in Afghanistan. Military aircraft and chartered civilian airliners could fly military personnel and civilians as well as essential supplies from a number of countries.

I traveled to Afghanistan and to Iraq on scheduled and chartered military flights, via the NATO air-bridge and on board of private aircraft either chartered, or owned and operated by my clients, respectively.

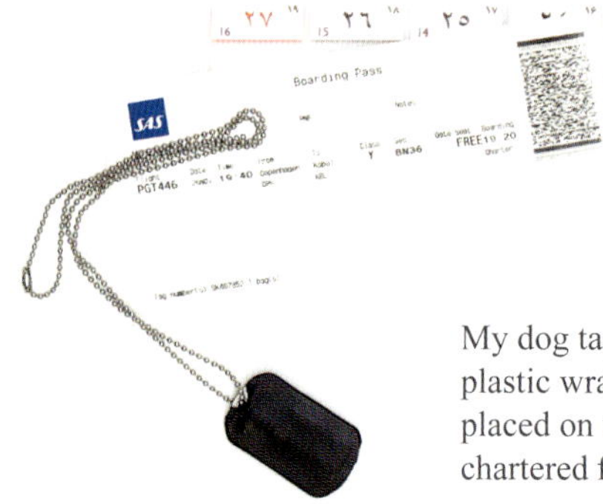

My dog tag and a small amulet in plastic wrap and on a bead chain, placed on the boarding pass for a chartered flight.

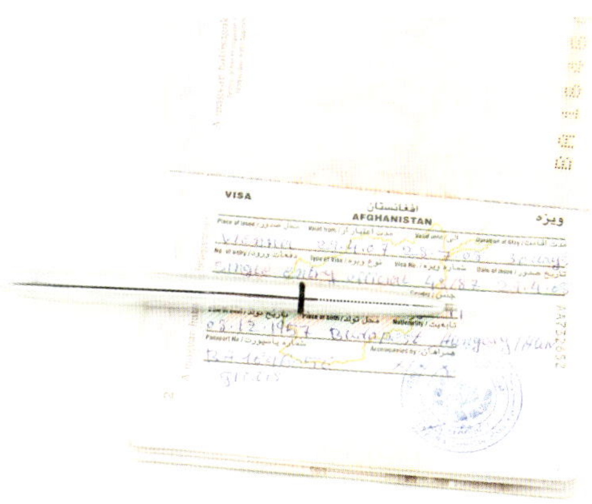

Afghan visas in different years.

En route to Afghanistan on board of a C17 Globemaster III transport aircraft, January 2011.

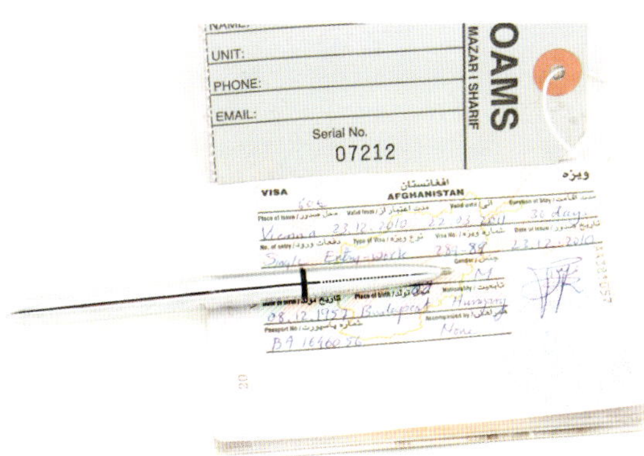

I received my first proper Afghan visa as late as 2006. I do not recall any paperwork in previous years.

Every time I traveled to Iraq, I received a proper Syrian visa. I had a stopover in Damascus and I was ferried to Baghdad by my client.

Syrian visas as well as entry and exit stamps when I worked in Iraq in different years.

Due to the nature of my assignments, I had a virtually unlimited weight allowance, since I had to carry everything to sustain my client … and myself. Each time, I carried a lot of stuff.

My gear stowed in the corridor upon my arrival. Living containers were placed in a row on either side of the corridor.

My personal gear before my departure from Afghanistan at the end of my contract in 2011. I left a huge amount of materials behind in safe storage on the premises of the PRT base in Pul-e Khumri, Baghlan Province. I never recovered a single item from that lot. The most painful loss was the mysterious disappearance of my beloved 9 mm Makarov pistol from the office safe of those who were supposed to guard and protect me and my gear. Such is life ...

I transported my equipment in sealed cardboard boxes. My personal gear traveled in a hard shell suitcase, or in a footlocker.

A footlocker is a trunk for storing personal belongings. In true military fashion, almost every regular soldier and contractor had a footlocker at the foot of his/her bed as in the barracks.

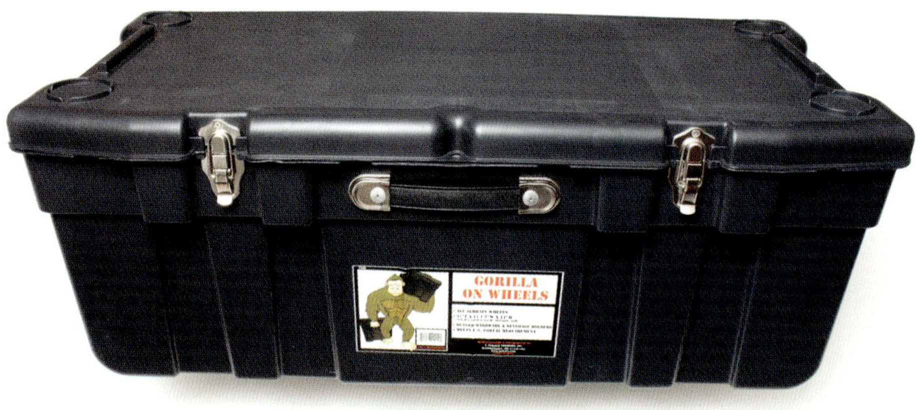

A footlocker, a.k.a. a PX trunk, holds tight under stress and impact. This footlocker has two heavy-duty wheels for transporting heavy gear.

Farewell to Afghanistan
On board the NATO air-bridge—a chartered flight from Mazar-e Sharif.

"Sir, I'm not aware of any such activity, or operation. Nor would I be disposed to discuss such an operation, if it did in fact exist, Sir." — Capt. Willard in Apocalypse Now (1979). Directed by: Francis Ford Coppola, distributed by United Artists.

43. Bringbacks: Mementos of My Tours in Iraq and Afghanistan

I brought back a lot of items, mementos of my tours in Iraq and Afghanistan.
My virtually unlimited weight allowance on scheduled and chartered military flights and private aircraft both to and from the theater of operations created excellent opportunities to enlarge my collection.

The first souvenir that I brought back from *Stan* was small and seemed insignificant at that time. Little did I know that the *Kulfa Ball*, which was a Pakistani-made coconut candy with Osama-bin-Laden and a missile on its packaging, would be followed by a trillion other bringbacks in the following ten years.

Right in the beginning I acquired an appetite for magnificent hand-painted and stenciled warning signs on metal plates, plywood panels, and on any other materials that their makers had access to. These and similar warning signs of all shapes, sizes, and color were posted on public buildings, on and near military bases, on the rear end of convoy vehicles, along the perimeter of known mine fields, and along roads all over Afghanistan and Iraq.

I never "liberated" any posted signs. Every time a sign caught my eye, I used a local "fixer," or an interpreter to obtain the same, or a similar one either from the same batch and from the same local sign painter, or from the same warehouse.

Now I admit, in one isolated case, I picked up one "keep distance" sign that "fell off a truck," namely the spare wheel of a HUMVEE truck.

Consequently, all other signs in my collection are in near mint condition, since they were never exposed to the elements.

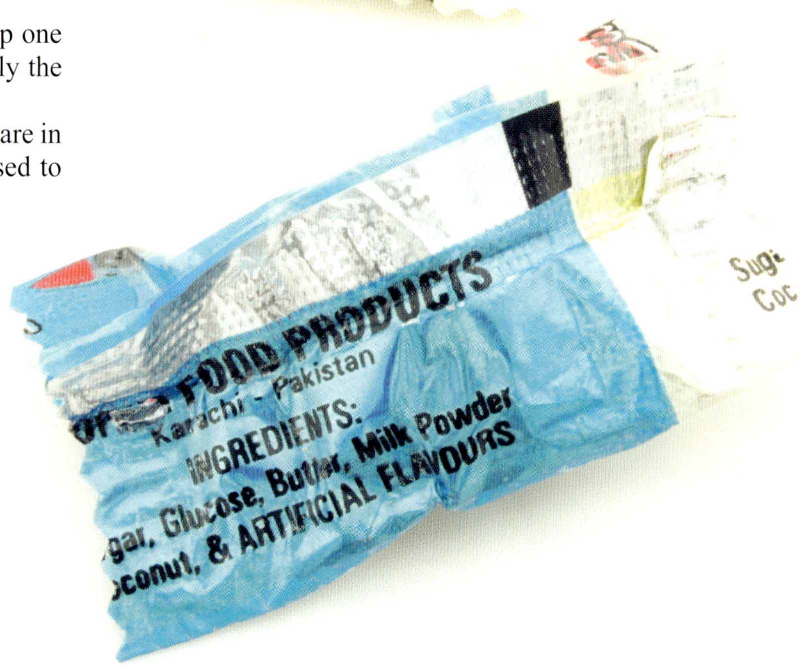

Black banner with the hand-painted *Shahada* in pure white in the *Nasq* calligraphic style. Manually applied oil paint on 100 % cotton fabric.

The two Black Banners with the *Shahada* come from a local calligraphy artist, a highly talented young Afghan man from Kabul. Both hand-painted banners are a testament to his calligraphic skills. Only my deep concern for his security prevents me from giving him due credit.

The larger black banner is "new old stock," a memento from the early days of Operation Enduring Freedom. It remained unclaimed for years, the client who ordered it never showed up and never paid for it.

The smaller one is a more recent item, which was created during the ISAF era in response to a constantly increasing demand for such banners.

Black Banner with the hand-painted *Shahada* with a wrist watch placed on the flag for size reference.

The Shahada, which literally means "testimony," is an Islamic creed. It is a declaration of a religious person's firm belief in the one God and Muhammad as God's prophet. The declaration in Arabic sounds like this: la ilaha illa-llah, muhammadur rasulu-llah. In English: There is no god but God. Muhammad is the messenger of God.

Black Banner with hand-painted *Shahada* in pure white in the *Nastaleeq* calligraphic style. Manually applied oil paint on synthetic fabric.

The Shahada is written in green on the top. The calligrapher's signature is in the top left corner. The black oil-painted Pashto text is: WELCOME TO AFGHANISTAN, THE COUNTRY OF PRIDE AND HONOR

Nangarhar Province (Jalalabad) Culture and Information Directorate is written in green in the bottom left corner.

This sign comes direct from the calligrapher's workshop. Similar welcoming signs were posted on a light blue heavy-gauge metal tube frame along the road. Alas, the frame was too bulky and I could not take it.

WELCOME TO AFGHANISTAN sign to be posted at the state border. Handwritten Pashto text on a spray painted aluminum sheet.

Cheap mass-produced digital watches

TIMEX Ironman Triathlon.

I bought the TIMEX Ironman Triathlon and the Casio F-91-W with a small compass on the original resin strap from a market trader in December 2008 in Kabul.

I had bought precious war rugs and portrait rugs from him before. The portrait rugs bore the images of well-known figures who had shaped the recent history of Afghanistan.

Maybe my familiarity with the role of these commanders in the troubled history of Afghanistan, maybe the prices that I paid for his rugs led him to believe that an unforeseen opportunity to sell two seemingly ordinary digital watches, which were meticulously wrapped in a *shemagh* and thus, to make a fortune, presented itself for him at last. He charged an astronomical price for the watches, which looked somehow familiar to me. While I completely disregarded his tale about the watches, I bargained his price down to less than half of his asking price and—with a little encouragement from my Afghan colleague who accompanied me on that day—I bought them.

Much to my surprise, the subsequent analysis of press photos and video interviews from the 1990s and the early 2000s, corroborated the seller's words and proved beyond any reasonable doubt that the same watch brands and the same models of watches even the same watch straps and the same small compass were worn by a famous, or rather notorious mujahid leader, the head of an international terrorist organization and the mastermind of countless attacks that cost the lives of a host of innocent people.

Casio F-91-W.

TIMEX Ironman Triathlon.

T-shirts

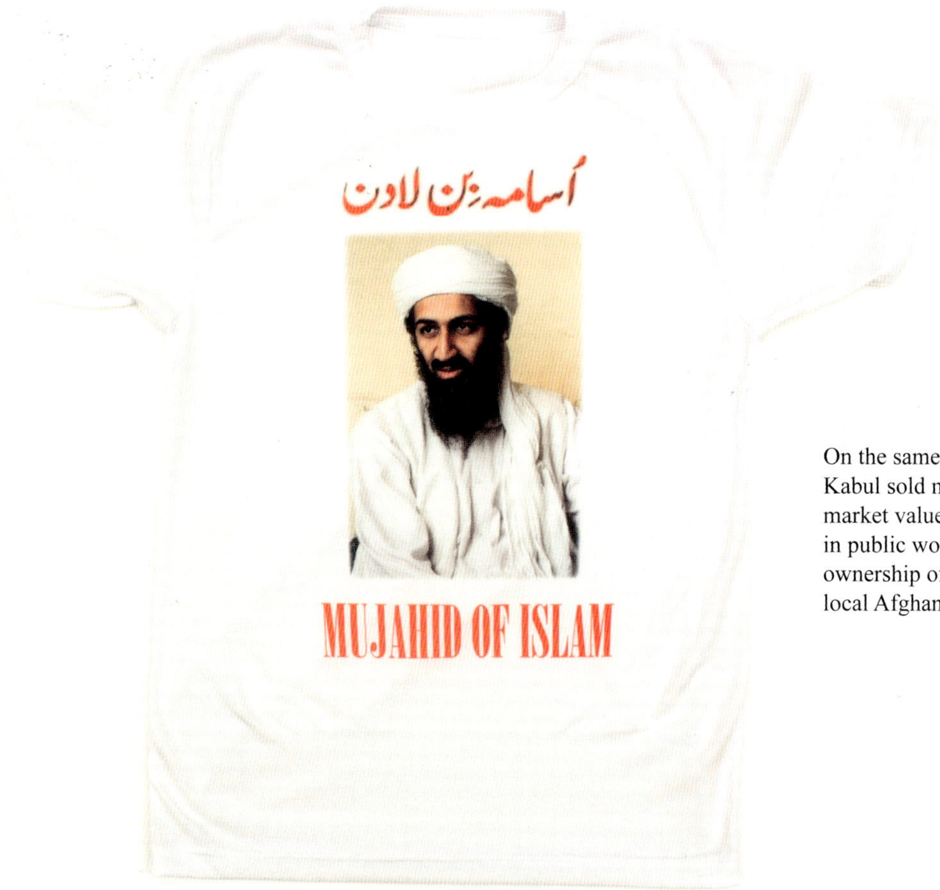

On the same day, the same market trader in Kabul sold me two T-shirts that had zero market value at a time when wearing them in public would have been suicide. Even the ownership of T-shirts like these could get a local Afghan man a one-way ticket to hell.

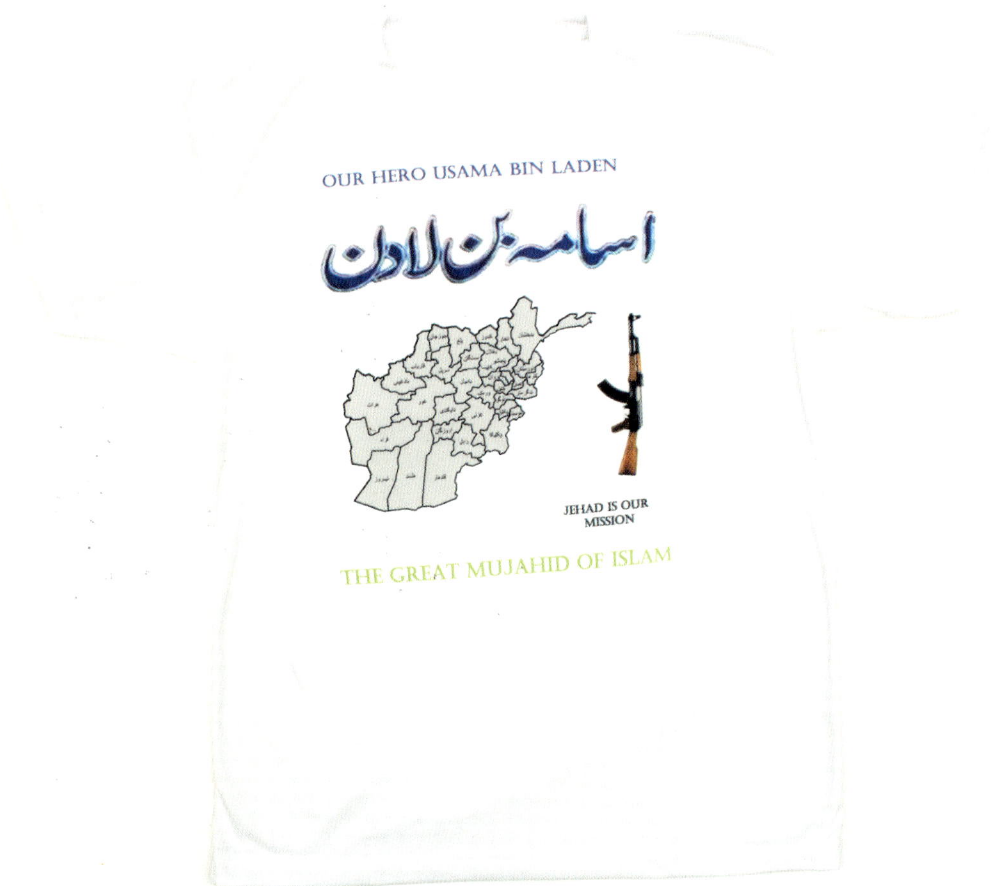

Nevertheless, he claimed they were worth their weight in gold. Luckily, cotton T-shirts do not weigh too much.

I bought another similar T-shirt in the main market near the *Chawk*, i.e. the big roundabout, in downtown Pul-e Khumri, Baghlan Province in 2011. I was working deeply embedded in the local community, I was wearing local clothes and I was shopping for *Zarbali*, the illegally distilled and secretly sold local booze when I spotted the T-shirt on a wire hanger in the back of a *ghorfa*, a small container shop. It was stained and worn and it showed some discoloration. Nevertheless, I bought it along with the highly coveted bottle a *Zarbali*.

Portrait Rugs and War Rugs

Portrait rug of Marshal Mohammad Qasim Fahim, knotted pure wool. Purchased in Kabul, 2008.

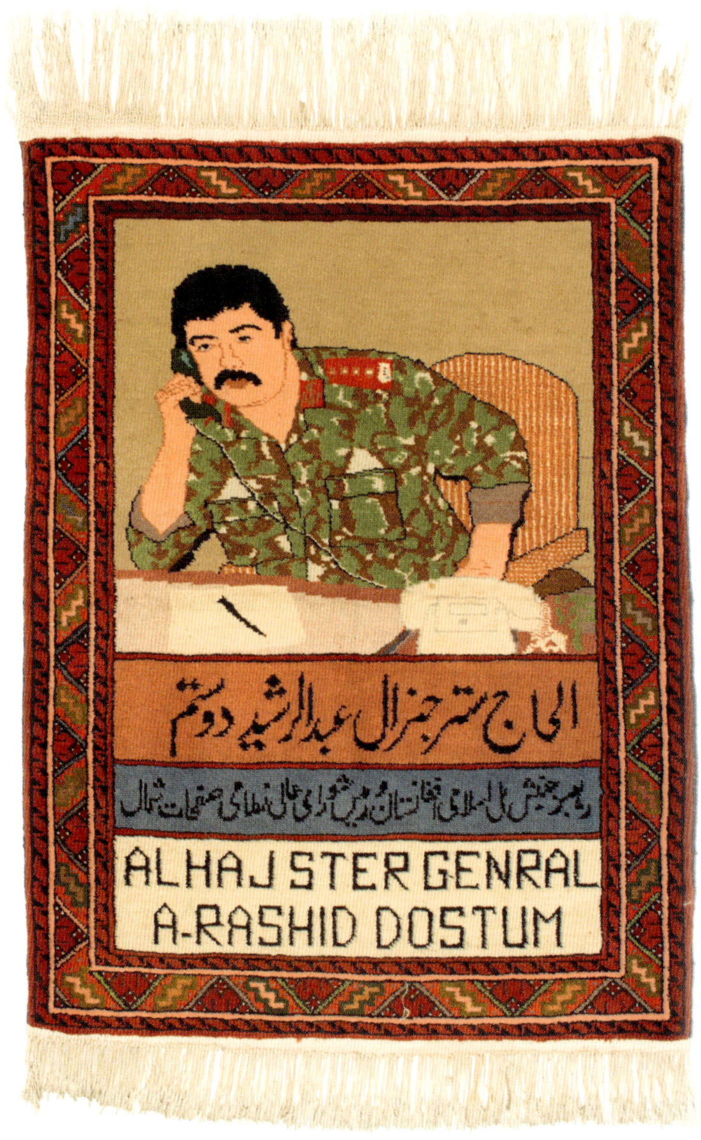

Portrait rug of Commander Abdul Rashid Dostum, knotted pure wool. Purchased in Kabul, 2008.

Portrait rug of Abdul Ali Mazari, knotted pure wool. Purchased in Mazar-e Sharif, Balkh Province, Afghanistan, 2011.

Portrait rug of Amanullah Khan, Amir, subsequently King of Afghanistan, knotted pure wool. Purchased in Mazar-e Sharif, Balkh Province, Afghanistan, 2011.

War Rugs
I built a fine collection of war rugs over a period of almost ten years. Some are presented on the inside cover pages, some are shown in this chapter. The majority of them are either on the floor in our sitting room, or in storage.

Mahny, our female Tazi dog (genuine Afghan hound) and her *KALASH* on a war rug

"First thing when he got home was that he rolled out the Afghan war rug that he had purchased in the bazaar on the floor. His dog occupied it instantly. She was an Afghan hound. Somehow, instinctively, she new the rug came from her ancient homeland. The call of the soft fabric was irresistible."
—Excerpts from *Zarbalistan: The Traveler's Ultimate Guide to Ariana,* by Zammis Schein.

The same rug and the same AK-47.

The same rug and the same AK-47 (detail). Folding stock 7.62 mm x 39 mm AK-47, dated 1955, with a matching slab side 30-round steel magazine.

The same rug on my cot in my room, which was a converted shipping container on an army base.

The same rug with *Dost* and *Ashty*, a happy Afghan hound couple.

Naan, i.e. Afghan bread, wrapped in pages detached from the ISAF magazine on a war rug that covered my cot in my room in Pul-e Khumri, Baghlan Province in 2011 and is on the inside cover of this book now.

On an other assignment I used another rug as a bed cover in my container room.

Mahny, our female Afghan hound is napping on a war rug.

The same rug.

The same rug (detail). A 7.62 mm x 39 mm AK-47 cartridge is placed on the magazine of the gun on the carpet for size reference.

Dost, our male Afghan is napping on a war rug.

The same rug.

Afghan carpet makers depicted 9/11 in their works of art.

A carpet maker's view of the air campaign that initiated the liberation of Afghanistan.

A Souvenir from My Assignment in 2011
Similarly to the overwhelming majority of war rugs, this one depicts the withdrawal of Soviet troops from Afghanistan in 1989. After several rounds of fierce bargaining and chatting with the market vendor about all sorts of fascinating topics, a small Afghan war rug cost the equivalent of $20 in the local market of a small rural town. Large ones might cost over $300. Obviously, prices in Kabul could have been much higher.

While everyone in his right mind would protect his magazines from dust and debris, cutting AK magazines open on one side and displaying the neatly stacked bullets has been fashionable among Afghan warriors. The 7.62 mm x 39 mm "bakelite" magazine with a bullet-shaped window on the right-hand side is a souvenir from a contract assignment in Tarin Kowt, Uruzgan Province, Afghanistan, in 2007.

This war rug depicts an AK with a "windowed" magazine. The 7.62x39 mm "bakelite" magazine with a bullet-shaped window on the right-hand side, is a souvenir from a contract assignment in Tarin Kowt, Uruzgan Province, Afghanistan, in 2007.

Cans of Soft Drink and Bottled Water
Dozens of different brands of ice cold soft drinks as well as bottled drinking water were freely available in the mess halls on military bases. Also, they were available in local markets and stores.

Soft drink bottled in Afghanistan with its original bottle cap.

In 2011 in Pul-e Khumri, Baghlan Province my taxi passed through a big intersection every day. I kept alternating routes in town, but I could not avoid this "choke point," where a blind beggar sat in the dust, or in the mud, or on icy snow between opposite lanes of traffic on each day of the year. He was a human wreck in the true sense of the word. Since my taxi was a left-hand drive vehicle and I usually sat in the back on the right side, I always asked my driver to pass a $1 note into his outstretched hand. I never had a chance to talk to him, but on the basis of the big grin on his face, I am sure he could tell Afghan and US bills apart by just touching them.

A cigarette lighter, purchased in the PX store, also doubles up as a bottle opener. This bottle was purchased from a roadside vendor for thirty Afghanis, the equivalent of $1 in 2005. With the passage of time the exchange rate had shifted towards AFN 45 to the US dollar by 2011. Local money changers treated even the latest series of $1 banknotes with contempt, since they were afraid of fakes.

Reward Matchbooks

Reward matchbooks were designed and distributed under the auspices of the US State Department's Reward for Justice program. Reward matchbooks were printed in different local languages. This one is in Pashto. The objective was to disseminate the message that a hefty reward would be granted to any one who discloses confidential information that leads to the capture of international terrorists.

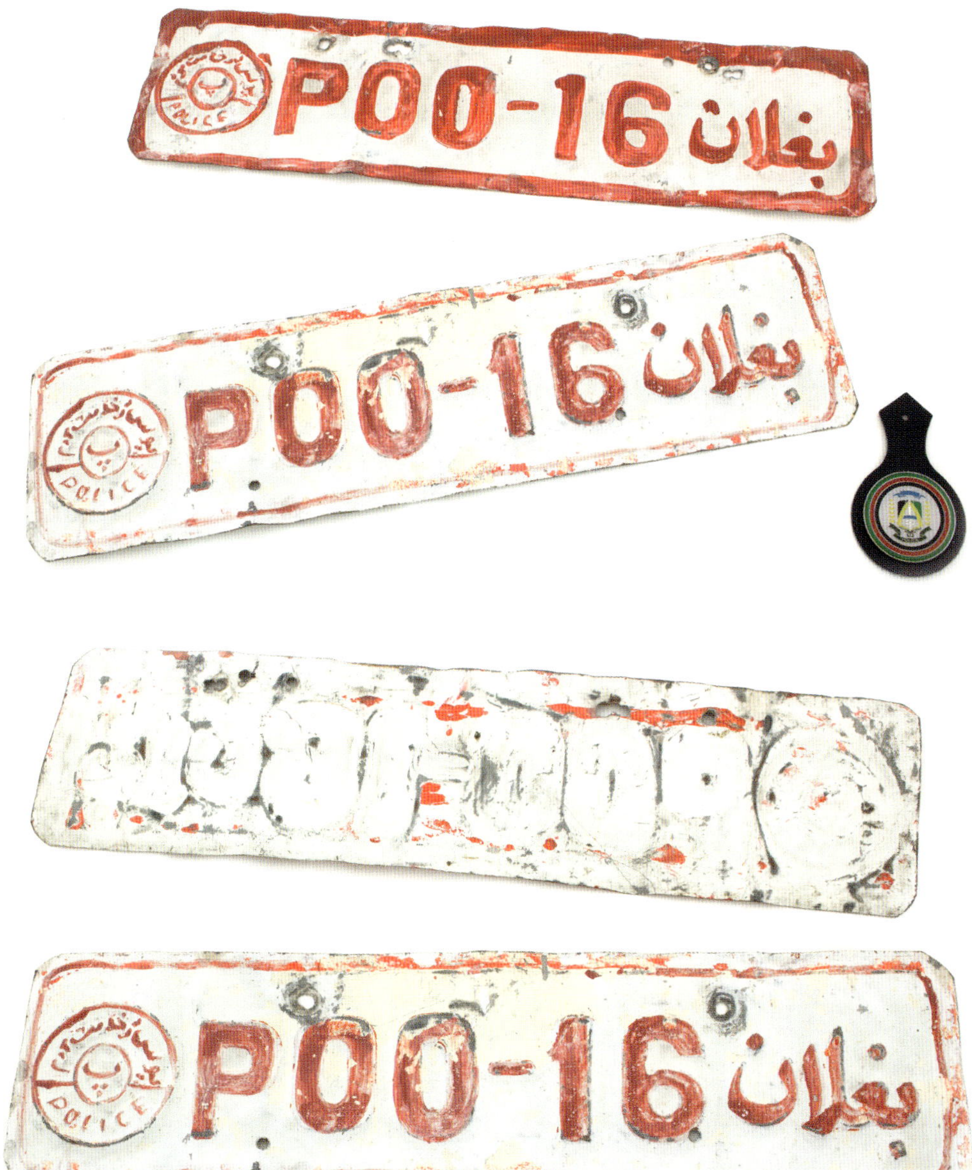

The pair of Afghan Police license plates look like something the cat dragged in. Actually, they are precious gifts from a high-ranking police officer who was kind enough to offer his office and his own prayer rug to Afghan trainee interpreters in my 2009 course who wanted to recite their prayers during the day, while they were in class.

He was in the head vehicle in a convoy when his pickup truck hit an IED, killing everyone else in a one-light year radius. Miraculously, he survived. All he could salvage from the still smoldering twisted frame of his police pickup truck were the heavily damaged license plates.

As a token of our friendship he gave me the license plates and his Afghan National Police pocket badge as a memento of that fateful day.

Afghan National Flags
Flags of various sizes were mounted on the antenna masts of ANP pickup trucks. The 7.62 mm x 54 mm round is used as a size reference, only.

CHECKPOINT Warning Sign
In order to give approaching motorists a fair warning, bilingual signs with pretty straightforward messages were posted ahead of checkpoints to inform drivers in time. Most warning signs were locally made and hand painted on whatever material was available. This item comes straight from a local sign painter's workshop in Basra, 2008. It is handpainted with oil paint on a white coated compressed fiber board.

SELLING NOT ALLOWED

This SELLING NOT ALLOWED sign was posted a few feet from the entrance to a shopping bazaar in the Green Zone in Baghdad.

Only licensed traders were allowed to sell their goods to mainly western customers, diplomats, military personnel, and contractors in the bazaar.

While it was a heavily controlled area, virtually everything in the whole world was available either officially, or under the counter. I could not comprehend why anyone would try to sell anything in the small square outside the designated area of the bazaar. Hence, my interest in this sign. Black stencil on a plywood board.

The AKM Assault Rifle on a NO WEAPON Sign

An AKM assault rifle is presented along with the same "NO WEAPON" sign. The sign shows a similar, but "Khyber Pass" AKM.

NO WEAPON Sign

The sign is one of a series of virtually identical signs made by a highly-talented sign painter in Kabul in 2004. The signs were intended for display at the entrance of city parks in downtown Kabul. I found this hand-painted sign especially interesting, because it shows a "Khyber Pass" variant of the AKM, which has a skeleton butt. Such locally manufactured rifles, or guns re-assembled from the parts and components of other weapons are not uncommon in Afghanistan. Oil paint on a zinc coated metal plate.

DANGER—STAY BACK Bilingual Warning Sign
A host of variants of this sign were mounted on military vehicles, mostly Humvees, as well as contractors' SUVs and pickups that traveled on public roads in Iraq. The signs instructed local motorists in English and Arabic to keep a safe distance.

There were no standard sizes, or standard layouts. Metal plates, materials from surplus shipping crates, chipwood, and plywood boards were hand painted, or stenciled.

However, in the majority of cases the size of a warning sign was adjusted to the diameter of a Humvee spare wheel, where most signs were mounted. Either holes were drilled into the four corners of the signs and they were fastened to the vehicles by a length of steel wire or a rope, or a larger hole was cut in the middle and the sign was bolted to the spare wheel.

The paint shop where it was made declared this warning sign "surplus" (by my request). Consequently, it has never been mounted. It belongs to a series of warning signs that were commissioned by a private military contractor firm. The signs were intended for SUVs and up-armored pickup trucks that were operated by the private military company on the roads of Iraq. The signs politely asks motorists in English and Arabic to keep a safe distance. Red and blue spray paint on fiber board.

DANGER—STAY BACK Bilingual Warning Sign
This is another variant of the DANGER—STAY BACK bilingual warning sign.

This one was obtained with the assistance of a local Iraqi colleague from the motor pool paint shop on LSA Anaconda in Iraq. It is still "new old stock." It has never been used.

It belongs to a large batch of warning signs that were commissioned by the Army and which were also used by private military contractors who were employed by the government's main engineering contractor. In the majority of cases these private security contractors were assigned convoy escort security missions on the most dangerous roads in the world.

Since the main contractor to the government had a multitude of different operations on and around this logistics base, vehicles bearing this and similar warning signs were a common sight all over Iraq in those days.

The signs were intended for military Humvees and SUVs operated by the contractor firm. Red, green and black spray paint on a heavy gauge steel plate.

ATTACK DOGS ON PATROL Warning Sign
Military working dogs were the real heroes of both OEF and OIF campaigns. Black spray paint on white painted fiber board

NO WEAPONS Warning Sign
An extremely colorful hand-painted warning sign, a real work of art featuring an Iraqi service pistol—a Beretta M1951 license-built in Iraq as the Tariq. "Check Qhadeqhaya" means no-weapons in the local Iraqi Kurdish dialect.

It was acquired in Arbil (Erbil), Kurdistan, Iraq, in 2008. This is one of a series of hand-painted signs that were intended for display in public buildings. There were similar signs with an assault rifle in the centre, or with a more generic pistol image, or with no weapon in the center at all. It's just a coincidence that my local interpreter and fixer managed to obtain this one from a local sign painter. Manually applied oil paint on a thick plywood board.

KEEP DISTANCE warning sign on the spare wheel of the Humvee right in front of me. Doshi, Baghlan Province, Afghanistan, 2008.

KEEP DISTANCE Warning Sign
This "liberated" sign used to be attached to the spare wheel of a Humvee with a metal chain.

The Dari word inside the STOP sign literally means STOP. On the left hand side, the Farsi characters under "50" are "mtr." Originally, the inscription on this *KEEP DISTANCE* warning sign must have been spray painted on a heavy-gauge aluminum plate. However, multiple coats of manually applied paint in several places suggest that minor damages as well as wear and tear were subsequently repaired to keep this warning sign in good shape.

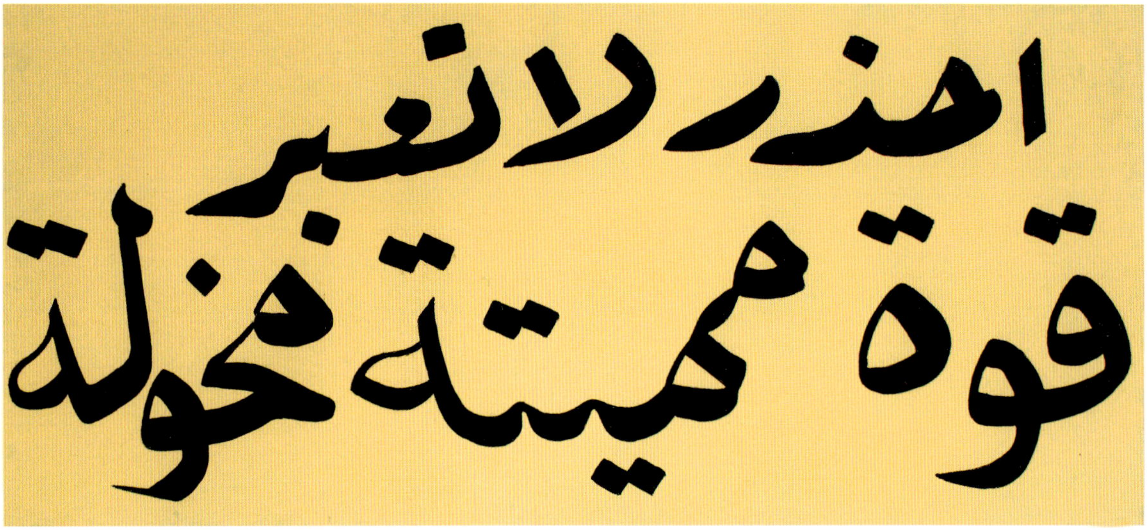

DANGER, DO NOT COME CLOSE—DEADLY FORCE WILL BE USED Warning Sign in Arabic

A warning sign was mounted on the back of a contractor's SUV. His team provided convoy security escort between LSA ANACONDA near Baghdad and FOB SPEICHER near Tikrit in Iraq.

Both side opening rear doors were removed and were replaced with two heavy gauge armor plates with a narrow gap between them. In this way, the rear gunner could cover a large area behind the vehicle.

"*Ahzar la tabar*" in the upper row means "danger, do not come close" and "*qoowata memyeta makhwala*" means "deadly force will be used."

The text is hand painted in shiny black oil paint, the background is painted shiny yellow. The sign painter's workshop made an honest effort to match the background color of this sign to the matt desert sand color of military Humvees and the almost identical shade of the contractor's vehicle. Oil paint on a heavy gauge aluminum plate.

COMPLACENCY KILLS Sign
"Trust no one. Complacency kills" … as the Marines say it.

Red spray painted stencil characters on a black painted wooden board. Acquired on Al Asad Air Base, Iraq, 2005.

Al Asad was not only a military base, but also a major logistics hub. Hundreds of truckers and private security contractors who escorted the convoys passed through it on a daly basis.

Minefield Marker Signs

Both Iraq and Afghanistan are infested with millions of land mines. Minefield marker signs are a common sight almost everywhere and unfortunately they are bound to remain an inseparable part of the heritage and landscape of the rural countryside in the future.

Some minefield marker signs are spot welded to metal rods and are driven into desert sand, or into the rocky ground, some are neatly suspended on wires that run along the perimeter of known minefields. For air transport safety reasons in Iraq, I was instructed to cut the lower half of each metal shaft with the sharp end off. I made up for the deficit on a subsequent assignment.

I never removed a posted warning sign from a mine field and I never hindered the heroic landmine and UXO clearance efforts of any of the NGOs and government -sponsored teams in Iraq or Afghanistan. Each minefield marker in my collection comes either from a workshop where they were made, or from a warehouse where they were stored.

Arabic language "skull and crossbones" minefield marker sign from Iraq. It is spray painted on a flaming red background. This is the only minefield marker sign in my collection that has a spray painted white rear side.

English Language Minefield Marker Sign from Iraq

Army stencil characters in white spray paint on a crudely painted red background. A full length metal shaft with the sharp end is placed next top the sign. At the end of a subsequent assignment I managed to bring one intact metal rod back.

The rear side of the same "skull and crossbones" minefield marker sign from Iraq.

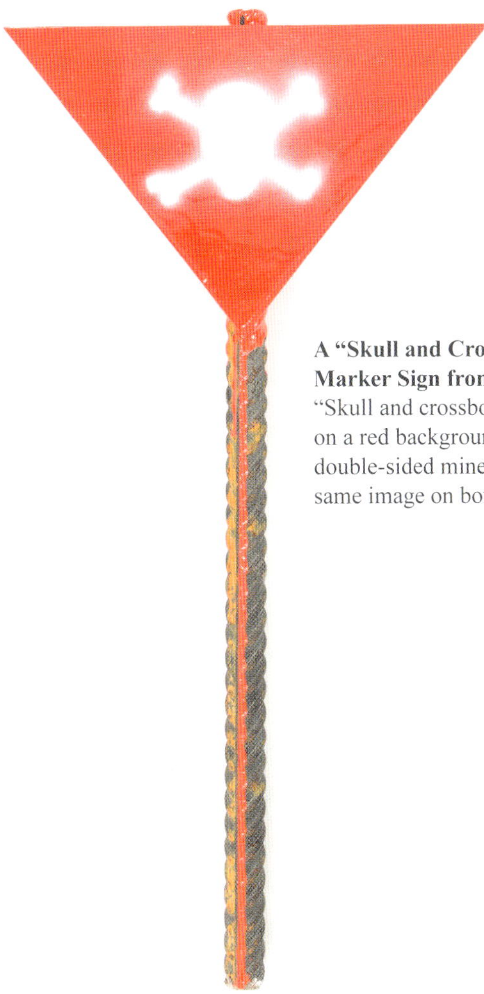

A "Skull and Crossbones" Minefield Marker Sign from Iraq
"Skull and crossbones" in white spray paint on a red background. This is the only double-sided minefield marker sign with the same image on both sides in my collection.

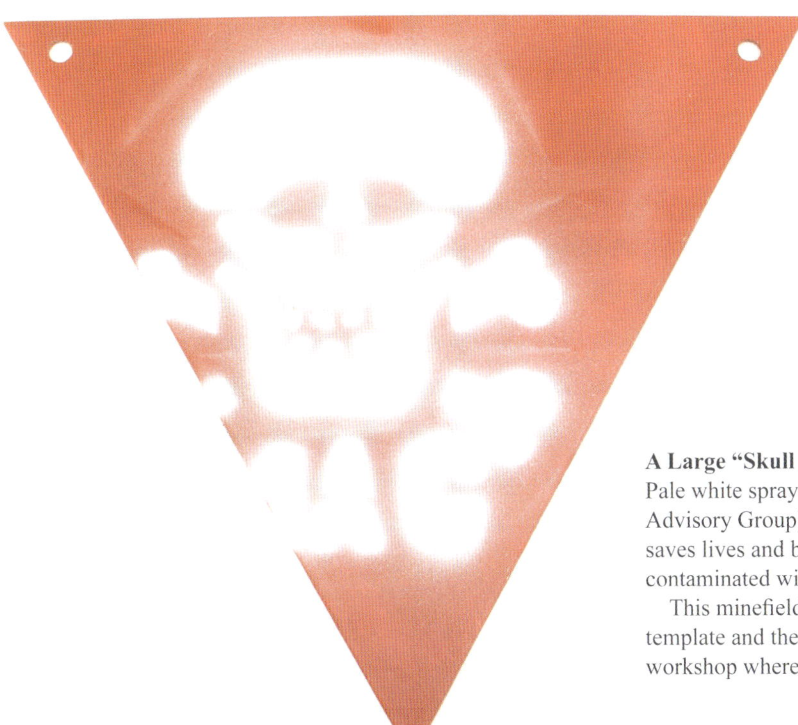

A Large "Skull and Crossbones" Sign from Iraq
Pale white spray paint on a dark red background. MAG (Mines Advisory Group) is an NGO that, "makes land and lives safe … saves lives and builds futures … by reclaiming land contaminated with the debris of conflict." I salute their efforts.

This minefield marker sign was scrapped due to a misplaced template and the substandard paintwork on it. It comes from the workshop where hundreds of identical signs were manufactured.

English–Dari Bilingual Minefield Marker Sign from Afghanistan
White spray paint on a flaming red background.

Arabic–English Bilingual Minefield Marker Sign from Iraq
White spray paint on a dark red background.

Afghanistan Football Jersey
It never belonged to the Afghan national eleven. All sorts of Afghanistan football jerseys were freely available in street markets and bazaars as long as there were foreigners, mostly soldiers, who bought them as souvenirs. It's a highly sophisticated replica. This one cost $10 while a less authentic-looking one would have cost the equivalent of $5.

This Afghanistan football jersey was purchased in the ISAF Camp Marmal bazaar in Mazar-e Sharif, Afghanistan in 2011.

The matching football shorts with an Afghanistan Football Federation patch.

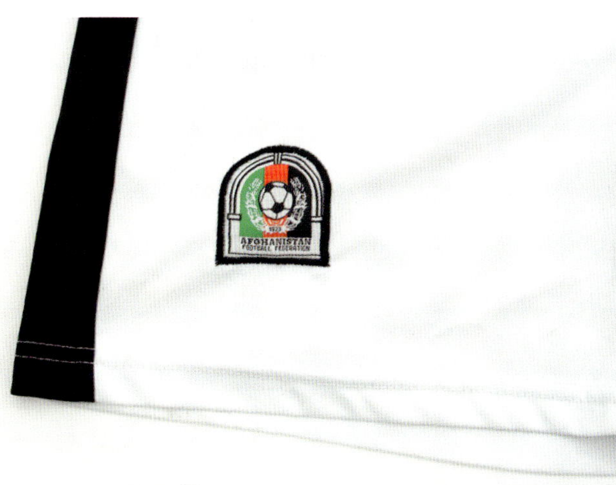

The *Shahada* is painted in golden-yellow in the *Nasq* calligraphic style on an ancient wooden board. A masterpiece by an Afghan calligrapher in Kabul.

Index

Other Schiffer Books by the Author:
Soviet and Mujahideen Uniforms, Clothing, and Equipment in the Soviet-Afghan War, 1979–1989 (978-0-7643-5115-0)

Other Schiffer Books on Related Subjects:
Modern Knives in Combat by Pohl & Schultze (978-0-7643-3766-6)
Double Action: Classic Revolvers for Target Shooting, Hunting, and Security by Ulrich Schwab (978-0-7643-4630-9)
Cold War Pistols of Czechoslovakia by James D. Brown (978-0-7643-3354-5)

Library of Congress Control Number: 2016958885

Type set in Trade Gothic LT Std/Times New Roman

ISBN: 978-0-7643-5258-4
Printed in China

Published by Schiffer Publishing, Ltd.
4880 Lower Valley Road
Atglen, PA 19310
Phone: (610) 593-1777; Fax: (610) 593-2002
E-mail: Info@schifferbooks.com

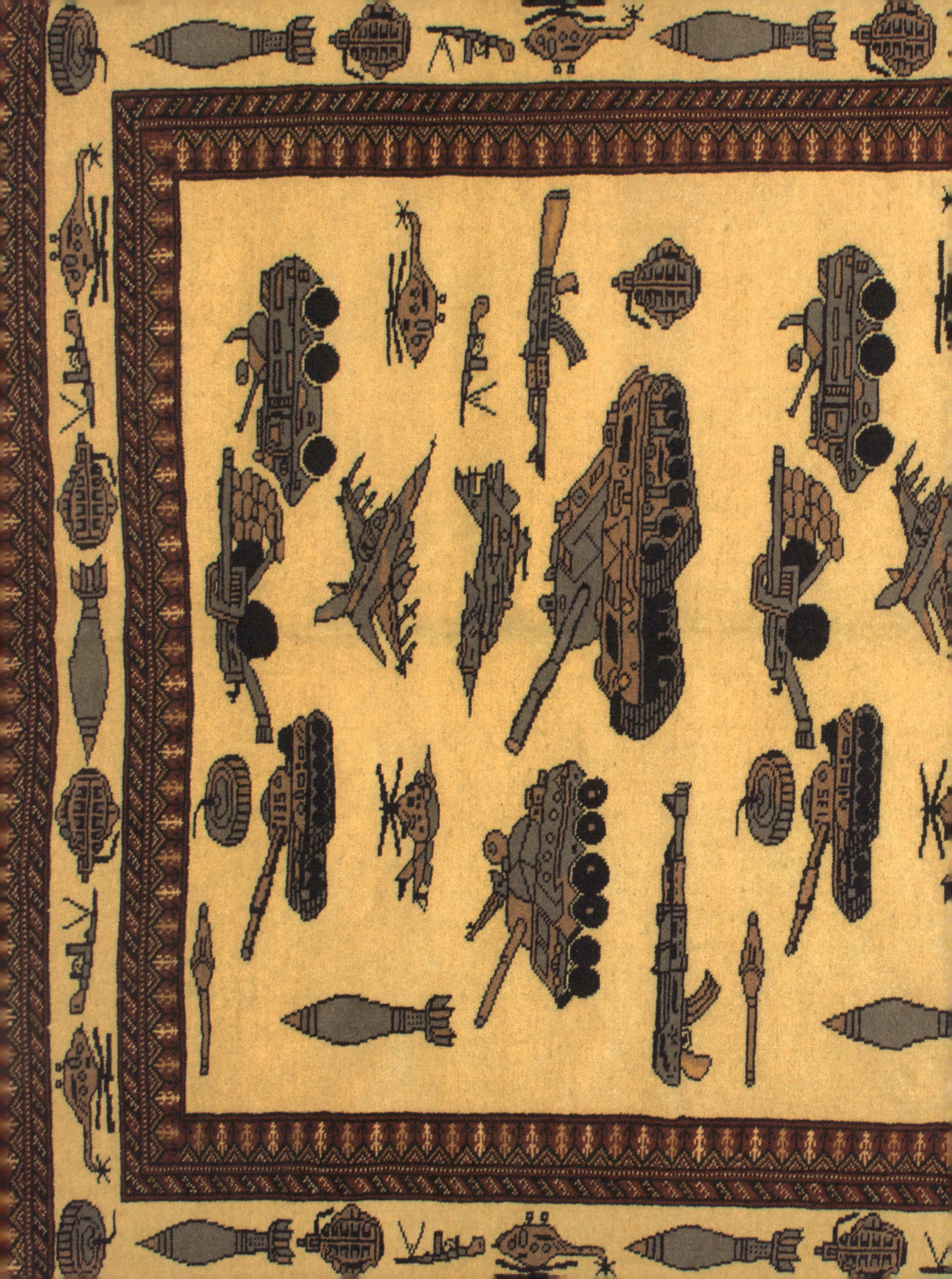